YOU CAN BE A Medium

How a **red couch** led me to mediumship
and turned my pain into purpose

TRACEY ESCOBAR

The Red Couch Medium

FRANKLIN ROSE
PUBLISHING

Publisher: Franklin Rose Publishing
www.FranklinRose.com

ISBN: 978-1-952146-16-9 (Paperback)
ISBN: 978-1-952146-17-6 (eBook)
Library of Congress Control Number: 2021910057

CONTENTS

For my father: Although our time together was short, I draw my strength, humor, and love of life from you and your Spirit! Thank you for showing me the magic and leading me to The Red Couch. I have found my purpose through your memory.

FOREWORD

In today's world, there is a greater curiosity and interest in the afterlife. People are beginning to realize that there is more than this physical experience and that our souls do live on. It has never been timelier to offer a book about understanding and exploring your gifts. Tracey Escobar does this wonderfully in her new book, You Can Be a Medium! I remember first working with Tracey, and her dedication to Spirit was undeniable. She would practice and train endlessly on perfecting her connection to the other side, and she has a level of integrity and authenticity that is unprecedented. Tracey would travel domestically and internationally to study with the world's best spiritual teachers so that she could hone and refine her gifts.

I remember having the honor of serving Spirit alongside Tracey in Dallas, Texas, prior to the pandemic shutdown. I remember her being nervous about the event. She wanted the event to be perfect! I simply told her to relax, be herself, and know that Spirit has chosen her to deliver those messages that evening. Needless to say, Tracey shone with Spirit all around her. Her personality made everyone feel at ease, and her specific information wowed many in attendance. Tracey is a remarkable medium, and she has never allowed her trauma to trap her. She understood that it was her path to follow and her journey to take. Tracey not only has maintained a professional demeanor but has continuously guided her students to open their gifts with her nurturing approach. She believes in each and every one of her students to fulfill their potential. She offers creative tools and exercises to stimulate and support her students to not only expand their gifts but to build their self-confidence. Tracey has come from being the student herself and working through her own fears, self-doubts, and past traumatic events, to become the master teacher to help her students discover their own red couch experience!

Tracey has always been a motivator, team player, and loyal asset to the spiritual community. She rallies all to come together for the sake of Spirit and does so with passion, empathy, and kindness. She has avoided many of the pitfalls lightworkers make along their journey and used her upbringing and trauma to offer hope to others. Spirit chose Tracey to not only serve them as a medium, but to put her in the spotlight to be a beacon of hope for others striving to change their lives and live their purpose. Tracey's book, You Can Be a Medium, offers a fresh take on how one can heal through their own personal trauma while exploring their gifts. She provides the guidance and support a student needs during their spiritual awakening. She provides a space of comfort with her vulnerability and openness to discuss her own experiences which opens the door for discussion and healing.

In You Can Be a Medium, Tracey shares her painful abuse and the trauma it created. She does this for the purpose of teaching that your trauma can be the trigger to your connection to Spirit, and she offers that ray of hope that you can absolutely not only heal from that trauma but thrive afterward! She certainly doesn't make light of the effort it takes to heal and the work one must put forth, but she offers a step-by-step guide in her book, setting the example of how one can radically change their life from pain, self-doubt, insecurity, and misalignment to fulfillment, joy, success, love, and acceptance! It is a great honor to not only be a mentor for Tracey, but to be able to call her friend and colleague! Her book You Can Be a Medium is your first step towards healing and spiritual awakening! Enjoy your red couch experience!

-Colby Rebel
International Psychic Medium,
Spiritual Teacher, and Author

PREFACE

Your gifts are like a rose unfolding.
You cannot force the bloom.
-John Holland

Can you cultivate psychic medium abilities?

Yes, you can.

This book is offered to you as a guide to plant the seeds and harvest your gifts so that you can do so. Believe in yourself, do the work, and be willing to be vulnerable. And it can happen.

I know this to be true—*firsthand.*

I was not born with the gift. I had to tend to my talents like a beautiful garden with patience, consistency, and the sweat of my brow. I had to nourish the soil, choose the right containers, and follow the sun. Now after many years, the blossoms fill my days.

This book shares my journey of becoming a psychic medium and growing the tools and practices that awakened my potential. I went from struggling with drug addiction, low self-esteem, financial issues, and little sense of meaning to discovering how to redesign my life and tap the greatest gifts of all: those sprung from Spirit.

You too can experience the life-changing transformation that I did. That is why I have written this book: I know if I can do it, *you* can too.

This book begins with my story—a childhood of abuse and trauma from which I had to heal to fully claim the gift. I share my past with the intention of inspiring you so that you know that no matter where you have come from, you are not limited in how far you can go. Take what is helpful in these pages and leave the rest. Your path will have its own magic, mystery, and pebbles along the way.

Some of you who are reading this may also have had sexual or emotional abuse in your childhood. Please be assured that traumas like these often offer unexpected abilities, especially in the area of psychic development; however, they also can cause the very wounds that keep us from our greatest potential as humans and psychic mediums. I offer tools for healing as well as psychic development that can show you that there is, indeed, purpose in your pain.

In my book, I will start by sharing my story and the path that took me to my first powerful spiritual affirmation of my calling—a red couch—and I will share with you how to discover what your true gifts are and how Spirit will guide you. I offer a series of exercises and practices that will make it possible for you to experience personal and psychic growth. I begin by exploring healing—how to tend to your emotional garden. Once you begin healing your roots, you can enjoy the fruits of these labors by tapping into the powers of Spirit to connect with the afterlife. I offer a series of practices that can mend the past and manifest your new expanded future.

Join me in discovering Eden.

It all starts with one red couch.

CHAPTER ONE

SOUL LESSONS

All things happen in their proper time. Everything in life happens in the time allocated for it. Don't waste energy worrying about end results. Worrying only distracts you from living day to day and enjoying life!
-James Van Praagh

My journey to the red couch was a long one.

Forty-five years, to be exact.

Throughout the decades, my soul has had many lessons.

Soul lessons. That's what I call them.

But it was well worth it.

I knew trauma and deep pain throughout my life. I spent decades suffering, feeling I was never seen, never good enough, desperate to be truly loved, and living in a state of constant fear.

The pain shaped me, changed me. Every soul lesson taught me acceptance, courage, patience, compassion, and most importantly, unconditional love. And in the end, I could see all I was truly capable of and who I was meant to be, who I was beneath the trauma, and how to help others find their own way through *their* soul lessons.

Did I choose these lessons before embarking on my soul journey to Earth?

Yes, I did. We all do.

At the same time, we are also in control of our own destiny, and our lives are in a constant state of co-creation. Ultimately, our souls' lessons all need to be learned, and it is our choices in this lifetime that determine how those lessons will be presented to us.

I chose the red couch. What about you?

Birth and Beginnings

On December 1, 1970, in the small West Texas town of Pecos, my little soul made the choice to experience life here on Earth. My mom was eighteen years old, and my dad was twenty-one. I was unplanned, perhaps even unwanted, as my young parents confronted the new, overwhelming reality of the pregnancy.

I felt their fears even as I was tucked away in the embryonic sac preparing for birth. Does trauma start in the womb? Yes, from what I have learned, even the fetus can tune into the emotional state of the parents. In those very formative months, soul lessons and human narratives take form as do our little fingers, toes, and lungs.

From the moment I could feel my mother's belly tighten with ambivalence, a narrative was set in place that determined the rest of my human story. This is true for all of us. Our destinies are determined from the moment we are conceived and as we gestate and then come through the birth canal into this world. Some babies come kicking and screaming; others bright-eyed, feeling an ease as they take the first breath. The fortunate newborns have mothers who welcome them in joy. But many of us feel the doubts, exhaustion, terrors of our mothers, and internalize the coolness of their first embrace as rejection. That was the case for me. The feelings of not being wanted and never being good enough then followed me after birth, throughout the decades, until I started on my path to mediumship.

In my story, I hope you will find insight into yours. What was the experience of your birth? Were you welcomed into this world? These are among the questions you might begin to ask in the pages ahead as we explore how to heal your life story as an important step to becoming a medium.

Abandonment and Generational Trauma

Although very young, my parents married before my birth—and then my father enlisted in the Army. He stood tall in his duty to family and country. A wide-shouldered man with a long, lean torso, buzz cut, and kind, sometimes dreamy, eyes, he looked handsome in his Army uniform as my mother, a frail beauty, hung onto him. They were young, attractive, . . . afraid.

And both had traumatic stories buried within.

My mom watched in terror as her mother died of cancer. Thirteen years old, still so young and vulnerable, my mom was left alone with her dad and brothers.

"You're the mama now," were among my grandmother's last words to her barely-teenage daughter. My mother became the woman of the house at a very young age, caring for her siblings years before she was ready to care for anyone. Then, suddenly at eighteen, she had her own baby on her lap. Just when she should have finally been breaking free to have her own life, I was sitting on her lap crying, reminding her that everyone's needs came before her own.

My dad also brought a legacy of trauma into the marriage. When he was four years old, his father was murdered, leaving his mother with little means to take care of her four young children. She had to make the painful decision to put her young ones up for adoption.

My dad and mother both experienced deep loss and grief with unexpected—even brutal—losses of their parents. These traumatic events, no doubt, had long-lasting emotional impacts on them, and eventually on me. Generational trauma is very real indeed, and clearly played a role in my fear of abandonment which led to deep isolation in my childhood years. Part of your journey will also be to identify the intergenerational, as well as the personal, traumas that have shaped your beliefs, attitudes, values, and life. Lifting these veils allows for greater clarity as a psychic and a medium; however, sometimes it is hard to recall the past.

Most of my early childhood memories were buried so deep within my consciousness that I have very few recollections. I understand now that memory loss can be a trauma response. I only have glimpses of my father screaming as I crouched behind the couch to hide from him as my mother cowered, shaking, struggling to muster the courage to scream back at him.

One day, drunk and longing for freedom, he wanted to go out to his favorite local bar, and my mom begged him to stay home with her. He pushed her, with all the strength of a soldier, and she flew back into the wall, crying in pain.

Alcohol destroyed my father's decency and his marriage. The smell followed him like a dark cloud and turned a once-handsome recruit into a pale, drawn man with bitter eyes. But like so many daughters, I still loved my father and wanted his approval.

Many days, when I was barely as tall as a barstool, I would walk into The Brass Asp, a smoke-filled, hole-in-the-wall bar next to our apartment, to fetch my dad. He would seat me next to him and order a cola with a cherry for me. Smiling happily, I would eat the cherries right out of the glass. We connected this way over a shot glass.

My parents ended up divorcing after the birth of my little brother. My father received orders and eventually moved to Germany. My mom worked full time, and she did the best she could to raise my brother and me. I am sure that being a young mom on her own, and not having her own mother available, was tough. My mom became a survivor. Unfortunately, she had little time to put attention on me, and I was given a lot of responsibilities at a very young age.

One day when I was eight years old, I was left to babysit my little brother and new baby sister. I remember my little sister, crying, "Juice. I want juice now."

"You can't have juice, baby girl—we're all out."

"I want it now. Give me juice!" She started crying the way toddlers often do.

I tried to quiet her, my anxious hands holding her close, but she squirmed in my arms, her screams intensifying. Just then, my brother spilled his crayons on the rug and started drawing on the wooden floorboards.

"Stop that! Mom's going to kill us if you do that!"

He wouldn't listen to me. I knew I would get in trouble if my mother saw the markings. I opened the window of our third-story apartment and just shrieked at the top of my little-girl lungs. Not a soul seemed to hear me or care. As I hung my head out the window, looking at the unresponsive world around me, the story continued: I was alone in the world. Nobody cared.

And how about you? What stories shaped your early years? What wounds have healed? What pains do you still carry?

Sexual Abuse and Secrets

Like so many children, I was sexually abused.

When I was eight, my mother remarried and had a baby—my little sister Cindy. We were now a family of five. My stepdad was also in the military, so we all eventually moved to Germany, where I spent my third, fourth, and fifth grades. I was finally in the same country as my biological dad and was able to visit him and re-establish our relationship. He had remarried, so I gained an additional stepsister, Melanie. They were happy, and I always felt welcome in their home. Growing up in Germany was remarkable. I learned a new language, traveled into beautiful new landscapes, and was immersed in the culture.

However, my time in Germany also had a dark side.

My stepdad and I had an easy-going relationship . . . until that night.

He had been drinking. I was asleep early, curled up on top of my blankets wearing a purple-and-cream-striped sweater and khaki pants. Startled, I felt his large hands scoop me out of bed, but I did not say anything and kept my eyes closed so he would think I was sleeping. He carried me into the dark room he shared with my mom. I could not see too much, but heard her quiet breath.

Frozen in fear, I continued to pretend I was asleep. Then he laid me in bed next to my mother. He had no clothes on and quickly unclothed me. He put one hand on his genitals and the other on mine. My body went numb, and I was scared to look at him except for brief glimpses to try to make sense of what was happening. Through half-opened eyes, I could see my mother sleeping with her back turned to us, her long, brown hair surrounding her shoulders, and her body rising and falling with each breath. My stepfather's hands moved in the dark. Petrified, I waited in sheer stillness for it all to end.

I kept this event secret for ten years, all while living with my abuser the entire time. Guilt and shame consumed me. I never wanted my mom to find out because I didn't want to hurt her; she deserved to be happy. I never wanted him to get into trouble— I loved him, in all the ways children do, as strange as that may sound.

However, I lived with hypervigilance, knowing that the abuse could happen again if I left myself vulnerable. In childhood and adolescence, I avoided his advances that included him asking me to come lie next to him on the couch, remarking about my body as I became a woman, secretly following me when I was out with friends, wanting to take photographs of me, and providing alcohol for me and my friends at our house. He was never hostile, but I always felt he was grooming me. He was solicitous and kind, so it was hard not to love him and even protect him, but I was also in a constant state of guarding myself, my mother, the family.

It was a huge burden for such a young person.

Young Love and Choices

When I started high school, my biological father moved back to Texas, where my mother and I were living again with my stepdad. My father and I built a great father/daughter relationship—playing sports, taking walks, talking about school and boyfriends. I was so happy to finally have my daddy back. During this time, I started to notice boys and seek out attention from them.

Looking back on it, I really just wanted someone to love me.

I met Adrian, my now-former husband. I was fourteen and a freshman, and he was seventeen and a senior in high school. He was my first love and sexual partner. Adrian came from his own dysfunctional family, ravished by mental illness and abuse. We were two kids in love who had no concept of how our early childhood trauma would play out in our adult lives, and how we would pass those traumas onto our own children.

Then, at the age of fifteen, in the summer of 1986, I found out that I was pregnant. After days of agonizing conversations, Adrian and I decided it was best to terminate the pregnancy. I announced this to my mom and stepdad, and they loaded me into the car and went to Adrian's house to discuss the abortion with his parents. Once again, life handed me more than I was ready to handle. I sat crumpled up on a couch, ashamed and afraid, as a room full of adults planned the details of the procedure.

"Of course, you will have nothing to do with that boy again, Tracey," my stepdad said as we got into the car to go home.

"Sure, Dad."

"No more dating him, you understand? You're too young to be making babies."

"Okay." I had no intention of doing what they said. I was fifteen and in love. "You're right, Mom."

On the day of the abortion, my mom took me to the clinic. Once we got there, we went inside to check in and go over the procedure. My mother's eyes darted nervously as she glanced around the clinic's waiting room. She looked like a small, helpless animal.

"I just can't stay, baby," she said. She broke into tears, holding her pocketbook close, shaking her head. "This is just too much for me now. You go ahead. They will take good care of you in there."

I did what I have always done: stood tall, didn't argue, and looked straight ahead when the nurse called my name. As the swinging doors opened, I entered those gray halls alone, knowing it had to be done, and that only I could do it. I was too young to be a mother, but I was doing something terrible, I felt. Regret filled every cell of my body as I waited for the doctor. The experience added more emotional trauma, more guilt, and more secrets to my short fifteen years of life.

Adrian went on to join the military after graduation and was gone for the remainder of my high school life. Although we wrote letters to each other, we were no longer together, and would remain apart until I turned nineteen. I had a normal high school experience after my freshman year: I was an honor student, played tennis and basketball, and was a flag girl for the band. I worked on the weekends when I didn't have games. I was mastering the art of hiding my traumas from the outside world. I had great friendships, and I even became homecoming queen my senior year. No one had any knowledge of the trauma I had suffered at home. I managed to live with my abuser while I kept all my secrets safely tucked away within. On the outside, I was the all-American girl—but on the inside, I was a lost, broken child.

Secrets Revealed and Reconnection

At nineteen, the secret finally came out about my sexual abuse. One of my closest friends told my mom. When I got home from work that day, my mom called me into the bedroom. When I walked in, my stepdad was sitting on the bed. My mom confronted me about the abuse in front of him. I confirmed what had happened, and he, of course, said he didn't remember anything because he had been drinking during that time. That's all I remember about that conversation, and I was not privy to any subsequent conversations between him and my mom. All I know is that soon after that, he took an overseas assignment with no intention of ever returning, leaving my mom alone, confused, and heartbroken.

At the time, I resented my mother's heartbreak. How could she cry over a man who had done such horrible things to me? I felt so angry and confused at her response, bitter as the full reality of my trauma hit me as an adult. It would take me years to process that resentment and get to a place of understanding. I know now that she was doing the best she could with the capacity she had. She wanted to be loved too. She didn't want to believe he would have done that. The life she knew had completely fallen apart. When we don't openly talk about feelings and emotions, it is easy to see things only from our perspective. From the perspective of the child within me, my mother was devastated over losing him, when, in reality, she was devastated over her world crashing and completely changing.

I would go on to care about my stepdad, even after he left. I continued to have contact with him occasionally, into my mid-twenties. The last time I saw him, we had breakfast at a truck stop, where we had a pleasant conversation, and he gave me money to help with Christmas for my children. It wasn't until my mid-thirties that I had the realization that what he did was not only wrong, but it was also criminal. It wasn't until then that I fully realized the trauma that I had suffered by his actions.

Adrian and I finally reunited when I was nineteen. We ran into each other at a local restaurant—the connection sparked, and destiny put us back together. I learned that he had returned home from Germany, was out of the Army, got married and had a son, and was now separated. We quickly picked up where we had left off four years earlier and began our relationship again. Fast, furious, passionate—I was all in, despite some unhealthy signs. I was so in love that I ignored every red flag. By April of 1990, I was pregnant again.

Death

April 1990 forever changed my life in another way as well. I was staying over at Adrian's house when I got the call from my mom to come home, and to hurry. I raced over there. My parents had been divorced for eleven years by this time, so I was not expecting to hear the words she was about to say. "Your dad has passed away."

"How, where, why, with who?" I asked as I scrambled to gather my thoughts. I was so young to have to face the death of a parent. How did a man in his forties, in good health, and only a month into his military retirement, pass away? How could this have happened?

My dad had decided to purchase property in the Odessa, Texas, area. He bought a home that came with a pecan farm. This was going to be his next chapter in life. He was going to run the pecan farm and live out his retirement. There was work that needed to be done on the house before he moved my stepmom, brothers, and sister to live there. He and one of his military friends went up a few weeks early to get the house in order.

On the morning of April 19, my aunt, who lived in the area, called to check on them. My dad answered the phone and said he wasn't feeling well and was going to sleep in a little more. That afternoon, when my aunt and uncle went to the property to check on my dad, they found him in bed. He had already passed away. They checked on my dad's friend who was in bed asleep. When it was difficult to wake him, they knew something was wrong with the house. We later learned that the night before, my dad had lit the pilot light on the house heater, and the latch did not close properly. Carbon monoxide had filled the house, causing the untimely passing of my dad. His friend, thankfully, survived because he was sleeping near a window that was not sealed well, and that bit of fresh air saved his life.

My father and I were far apart during my young life, such as the years he was in Germany and I was still in Texas, so our contact became little more than letters, but I have to say my connection with my dad had never faltered. I always felt a strong connection to him. Always. And suddenly, he was gone.

I was nineteen years old at the time, and this would be my first experience with death and grief. My dad and I were not on the best of terms at the time of his passing. It was normal father-daughter teenage stuff. Never, in a million years, did I expect not to ever see him again or to not have an opportunity to say I was sorry. I struggled with guilt and anger for many years. Guilt for all things left unsaid, and anger at him for leaving me at a crucial time in my life and not being able to meet his first grandchild who was coming that December. I never even had the chance to tell him I was pregnant.

I was hurt and angry that he did not visit me in a dream. I can remember family members speaking of dreams they had about him after his death or watches stopping at a certain time. Why wasn't I having those same experiences?

This was the first time I really thought of an afterlife, or of what happens to us when we die. I found myself craving the outreach of my dad from the afterlife and being angry because it never happened. I was years away from realizing that I had the ability to reach out to him, to help heal my own loss. I was desperately waiting for him to come to me, and instead heard nothing. This silence only added to the lack of self-worth and the need for love that I felt.

Once again, I felt invisible.

Toxic Relationship

After my dad passed away, life went on. By this time, I had already suffered greatly from being the daughter of an alcoholic, coming from a broken family because of divorce, being molested by a trusted family member, and then being pregnant at nineteen with my first child. This was the point in my life when I decided to run away from my feelings and numb myself out. I would spend the next twenty-five years just trying to survive the rest of my life.

Adrian and I had begun a nineteen-year toxic cycle of breaking up and getting back together again. I went through my first pregnancy alone as he was having a baby with another woman. The baby was born just six months after mine. I lived for years carrying the heart-wrenching knowledge of his other child. (He didn't want our kids to know about her.)

This was yet another secret for me to conceal, more trauma to push down and file away. Adrian and I reunited, had a second child, and broke up again. He suffered from post-traumatic stress disorder

(PTSD) from his childhood and military service, as well as, we later learned, from mental illness. I became a single mother of two, supporting my family as a cocktail waitress and falling into drugs to self-medicate—and yet, Adrian and I always got back together.

I came from a broken home. I lacked self-love and self-respect. I had always wished to have a happy family of my own. I hoped that I would never get divorced like my parents did. I kept returning to Adrian, and he kept returning to me. We loved each other for a long time, but we were both damaged people trying our hardest to overcome the buried pain and broken experiences of love.

It was an unhealthy relationship, but it was all I knew, and it was mine.

At the age of twenty-five, I felt restless to escape my hometown. Hoping to start over somewhere else, I sold everything I had and told Adrian I was leaving with the girls and moving to California. My friend, Yvette, had two children as well, and was also in an unhealthy relationship, so we packed our cars and our children and set forth on a road trip to San Diego. Our plans there quickly failed. Yvette had once lived in Sacramento and had family there that she thought could help us, so we hit the road again.

While we were there, both our husbands decided to sell all their possessions and met us in Sacramento. With the last $100 we had, we found a move-in special for an apartment. We finally had a home again—an empty home, but a home, nevertheless. The apartment manager gave us a mat to sleep on because he felt so bad for us. We literally started over from nothing. Not long after that, I was pregnant with my third child, Christian.

Although my Sacramento experience was rough, I would never change a thing about it. That is where I grew up from being a young adult, trying to figure it out, into a mom of three beautiful children. Adrian and I both found jobs that would eventually become our careers. Our relationship continued to be a rollercoaster. I had nowhere left to run to, so I felt I had to stay and make my family work.

In Sacramento, mental illness struck my family. We learned that Adrian was bipolar. Now everything made sense—why he was always quick to anger, held grudges, and was often bothered by the smallest of things. I had become accustomed to walking on eggshells all the time, trying not to set him off. We had answers, but no solutions.

In the midst of this, I started my relationship with antidepressants. Being a young mom to three kids, working full time, and having a husband with mental illness, took its toll on me. My depression was so gripping that I knew I needed help. The weight of responsibility was crushing my spirit. My doctor decided that Paxil would be the best drug for me, and I started a regimen of antidepressants that would last for the next twenty years.

Sacramento was home to us for four years; then, we moved back to Texas to be closer to family. After we returned to Texas, we spent the next nine years raising our three kids, buying our first home, and becoming a sports family. By all outward appearances, I was a soccer mom with a great life. No one suspected that I also had to manage a toxic love relationship.

Adrian would continue to struggle with his mental illness. Managing his anger became a part of my daily life. I lived in constant fear of making mistakes: I had to be the perfect wife, mother, employee, and lover. I struggled with depression and the side effects of the anti-depressants, including an eighty-pound weight gain. My marriage, depression, and body were literally weighing me down.

Towards the end of our now-loveless marriage, it took everything I had to simply stay alive. I was always thinking that I just wasn't good enough. I even had weight-loss surgery, thinking that it would solve my problems and that I would be lovable then. But it had the opposite effect: Adrian resented me for spending the money, and I became more insecure and even more controlling. I remember a time when my soccer-mom friends were getting together for a happy hour. I had made plans to go with them and was getting ready. When I told Adrian, he forbade me to go. We got into a huge argument, and I ended up on the floor in my closet, calling my friends, crying, because I couldn't go. He came into the closet and threw his phone at me. I was in pain, and he responded with violence. I needed love, and he had only anger to give. I knew then that I had to find a way out. To the outside world, we were a perfect family. Only my truly close friends knew what was really going on. I knew that if I stayed, my soul was going to die. *I* was going to die.

Mediums and Psychic Potential

It was during this time that John Edwards and Sylvia Browne became influences in my life. John Edwards, in particular, filled me with awe. I wanted to be like him and possess his amazing gift. I remember praying for it and asking God why he didn't give me the ability to touch the divine, to feel such love and certainty. Part of me already knew that I could help people through mediumship. I saw a future in which I could share with others things that I still desperately needed myself.

I found some Sylvia Browne books and recordings on how to strengthen one's psychic gifts and abilities. I bought them all! Hidden away and locked in the bathroom, I would listen to her tapes. I had to hide from my husband, who was raised Catholic and didn't believe in psychics, and the children. I would listen closely and practice what she said at every opportunity. I felt a pull, a calling, that was leading me towards the answers I was seeking at the time.

In her teachings, Browne said to just practice on things throughout the day, so I did. One day as I was driving to work, I was listening to the radio and a contest came on. The question was: Who can guess the birthday of a guest that they were having on their show that day? Out loud in my car, I uttered a date. A few minutes later, the radio announced the date, and it was the one I had said. How on earth did I get that right? It seemed impossible. Were my abilities really starting to manifest? Could I have the gift?

By this time, my grandmother had passed away, and I wanted so badly to reconnect with her. Using Sylvia Browne's teachings, I was able to have a beautiful experience in a dream state where I met my grandmother's Spirit in a courtyard. She sat down next to me, looked directly at me, and winked. The wink was so significant to me because that was my last memory of her. She had gotten

Alzheimer's and was forgetting who people were. The last time I saw her, she looked at me and just winked. It said to me "Yes, my soul knows who you are." It was a beautiful psychic experience, but it was the last one I would have for another twelve years. I had much more to experience before I was ready to embrace Spirit and all that came with it. I had to first find a pathway out of my old life.

The Affair and a Way Out

Codependency has very real effects. It convinced me that I could not make it on my own and I was unlovable, so no one else would ever want me. My codependent self-talk nagged at me: "This is the best that life will ever get."

But then one day, someone came into my life who thought I was beautiful and perfect just the way I was.

He was easy to talk to. He gave me the attention that I was so desperately craving for my entire life. He was someone who saw me, heard me, and wanted me. He was in a similar situation to my own—on his way out of a marriage. Most importantly, he felt safe. At least that's what my broken, shattered, and empty self thought at the time. We met and had an intense love affair.

This man became the love of my life. He became my very best friend. He made me feel safe and secure—feelings I had been denied for far too long. I thought he could save me from my responsibilities, secrets, and trauma. If I had known then what I know now, I would have realized that he was as broken as I was.

We were just two broken people in love.

Shortly after our relationship became public, his teenage children stopped talking to him. We broke up two families, and for that I will always be sorry. Guilt, lies, and betrayal would eventually end our relationship, but I would spend fifteen years loving him unconditionally. Our relationship was never normal. I allowed myself to be invisible again for the sake of his wife.

I allowed our love to only be expressed behind closed doors, once again feeling unheard and unseen. During this time, my soul went through so much growth. I went spiraling into pill addiction. I was having severe back issues, and I had been prescribed Hydrocodone to help manage the pain and Ambien to help with sleep. I had had two back surgeries, gall bladder removal surgery, two weight-loss surgeries, and foot surgery all in the course of seven years. Hydrocodone and Ambien became my escape.

We all have people who come into our lives for a reason, a season, or a lesson. This man was all three for me. The reason was to help me out of a toxic marriage; the season was the chapter of my life that would break me the hardest, yet cause me to heal; and the lesson was unconditional love.

Even though he caused me pain, my healing has helped me to understand that people don't do things to hurt *you*—they do things because *they* are hurting. My relationship with him was an important step in my journey, but it did not take me to the other side just yet.

Waking Up

I continued to struggle. I was raising teenage kids on my own and had a difficult co-parenting relationship with Adrian. I had work, family, and health problems, and was carrying a lifetime of pain—and I had not yet learned how to release it. I was doing everything on my own, and pills became my solution *and* my problem. I was doing Ambien not only at night, but during the day. I became very self-destructive and could have easily killed myself or someone else. I wasn't living. I was merely existing.

One day I made a road trip to see my daughter. I was staring out at the long, flat road ahead of me, lulled by the hypnotic rhythm of the tires. Slowly, the thin, white line faded into darkness, and I collapsed into sleep under the effects of chronic Ambien use. I slipped into slumber while driving. Crash! When I opened my eyes, my heart beat quickly as I shuddered, shaking off the impact as I came back to awareness. I ran off the road into a shallow ravine at the side of the asphalt.

"Oh, shit. That was a close call! It could have all ended there."

I looked around me at the expanse of sky, the wheat-gold fields, and barren blacktop. Luckily, I was alone. No one saw me. No one was hurt. My racing, frightened heart was the only sound I could hear.

"This is out of control," I thought to myself. "Something has to change."

My daughter's best friend had been killed by a drunk driver. There was no way I would ever want to put anyone, including myself, at risk. Something had to change.

I was tired of living my life. Tired of *how* I was living my life. All I was doing was surviving—day in and day out. At work, I performed hard, demonstrating that I was a great employee, but I was struggling. As soon as I got off work, I wanted to do drugs; it was a constant battle. I had prescriptions going at three different places in different people's names. I was forty-five years old, numbing, running, and hiding from pain as much as I possibly could—and I was tired of it.

And then . . . a miracle.

I'll never forget the date—as the sun was rising on November 15, 2015, and I was just waking up, I heard a voice speak to me clearly, loudly, "Okay, no more. You are meant to be so much greater than you are right now."

The voice literally woke me up that day, and I was different.

I rose from bed with incredible energy—and felt as if I could run a marathon. It was divine vitality, emerging from the core of me like a fountain. I knew then that I would never be the same. My life was about to change. I knew that I needed to start seeking knowledge and getting answers. I chose in that moment to end the cycle of hurt and start my healing journey.

I sensed that my father, divine Spirit, and all my guides swooped in that day and said, "Okay, enough suffering."

That's what I tell people now who come to me, "Enough suffering. Let's get you on the right path, where you were supposed to be this whole time."

I decided, "That's it. I am going to start healing. I am tired of just living. I need it to be more than this." I felt this from deep within my soul.

I walked to the bathroom as if an invisible hand was pushing me. I reached for my red lipstick, and there—in a bright shade of red—I scribbled the words I would never forget. Guided by a whisper inside me, my first affirmation on the medicine cabinet mirror was, "You are meant to be greater than you are."

And then, my healing journey began. After that day, I never touched drugs again.

CHAPTER TWO

THE HEALING JOURNEY

We have all been placed on this earth to discover our own path,
and we will never be happy if we live someone else's idea of life.
-James Van Praagh

Mediumship is a calling; it is a journey that your soul desires.

To be the best medium you can be, you must heal your soul. You must touch the Spirit within you. You must go within yourself, move through your pain, and heal the broken child inside. Spiritual development will be a core component of your mediumship. You're building a relationship with your Creator, your God source. As you move through your healing, you will be reaching into the depths of your soul to discover your truth, your knowledge, and the love within.

You have got to reach deep to find the place where your soul is whole and complete. Everyone has two halves of themselves that exist side by side. You have your human story—this current version of you made of your mind, body, and everything you have experienced. And you have your soul, which exists within you and connects you to a higher realm, and that is the infinite in you that is with you every step of the way. Healing, and mediumship especially, is about connecting these two sides, bringing them together, and finding that wholeness. It is about allowing your higher self and the light and love within you to work to heal your pain, so you can live a more beautiful and healthy life.

Healing asks us to go within, to see life and lessons clearly—and let go. The stronger you connect to Spirit, the more you can transform your life. The more you heal, the stronger your connection to Spirit. It takes time to accomplish, but there is nothing better for your life and your work than spiritual healing. Love, healing, and happiness are always accessible; allow them to shine through.

I've found a few useful strategies and routines along the way that have aided me on my healing journey that I'm going to share with you.

Some of these tools may be useful to you as you begin to look at your life story, healing the pieces that may still be fractured, and mending for greater mediumship and a more inspiring life.

Church

Once I had awakened, I started seeking knowledge and answers. I had all these questions about my life and my journey—where I was going and my relationship to Spirit. In my quest for knowledge and truth, I began attending church.

I had gone to church occasionally throughout my life, but never with any real commitment. My grandmother would take us to church and Sunday school during her visits when I was little, and we went sporadically during my marriage. I always enjoyed attending services because there was this sense of peace I felt there that was missing from much of my life.

At the start of my awakening, I began going to church on my own—every possible chance. This new-found energy never left my body, and church was one of the places that I channeled it. I was merely seeking knowledge at this point and knew that there was something more for me. I had an awakening experience and had been gifted incredible energy for some purpose, but I wasn't yet sure what it was. I was looking for answers, but I think what I was really looking for was a connection to Spirit—I just didn't know it yet. Going to church felt like going to a place of Spirit. I was guided there so I could take the next step in my journey towards deepening my connection to Spirit and expanding my psychic potential.

I went to a grand church in Frisco, Texas; we have big mega-churches here. They are very charismatic in their sermons and their music, even featuring live rock-and-roll bands. These churches are filled with energy. The church I went to had an amazing pastor, who is very much like a prophet himself—a super charismatic man, larger than life. He was very tall and muscular—he was once on a weightlifting team. With his commanding stature, salt-and-pepper beard, and piercing blue eyes, the pastor was a force to be reckoned with as a man of God, and he was very well respected. He nearly died once as a child, and his near-death experience awakened in him a deep connection to Source.

I had my first real experience of Spirit in his church. I had some idea about Spirit, but nothing more. If you've ever been touched spiritually in this way, you know how powerful it can be: overwhelming yet still comforting, filled with light and energy, but also touching peace. It can feel like something infinite and true in a world full of fleeting and false truths that often lead one astray. It was an experience that stayed with me and changed me forever, and has done the same for many others. I felt it as if it were the presence of God or Jesus: as though the presence was in me and went through me. That was my first true experience of feeling the supernatural.

That day, when I was hearing the message and was actually able to speak in tongues, was an awakening for me. We were all sitting there at the end of the midday service, wrapping things up. The band was playing these newer, trendier hymns. People were up on the stage, singing, swaying, and we were all singing along with them. With eyes closed, I rocked back and forth in my seat, listening to the pastor's powerful, prayerful words. They were reaching me, and I was deeply immersed in the experience. A spiritual presence that I couldn't explain was reaching inside me and connecting to me in a profound way. Then . . . I just let go.

When people carry around shame and fear as much as I did, they are often very reserved. I never wanted to be open around people because I had experienced so much trauma in my life and had secrets and low self-esteem that I tried to manage and hide from others. Vulnerability is difficult for most of us. The more we have been hurt, the more we learn to keep our guard up so we appear to be strong rather than appearing weak. Vulnerability asks for something completely different of us. Emotional and spiritual vulnerability require that we let our guard down and allow our-selves to accept what is.

And on that day, probably for the first time in my life, I surrendered.

I let go. I cried out in my head, "Help me. Show me what I am supposed to do." It was a beautiful moment of finally crying out for help. I surrendered to the experience, to my vulnerability, and to Spirit. For the very first time, I let my lips move and my tongue move, and I just spoke, and whatever came out, came out, and I didn't care. I was completely open. I went deep into the experi-ence and was able to just surrender. It was shocking to me because I felt as if my very soul was being touched. I was feeling the Holy Ghost, and what I really felt was mediumship. I felt the Spirit, and, in that moment, the truth came over me that everything is going to be okay.

When I left church that afternoon, I was transformed. I felt the supernatural finally becoming a presence in my life, and it felt genuine and real. Spirit was finally a positive, tangible presence in my life. I had touched, and been touched, by Spirit—and a whole other world was about to open up to me.

My seeking led me to church, and the church led me to experi-encing that feeling of Spirit as a real and powerful force, as some-thing more than an idea. Up until that point, I hadn't ever felt my dad. If he was trying to contact me, I didn't know what to expect or what to look for. So, I think that experience of feeling Spirit brought joy to me because I could now pinpoint it. The first time it happened was with God or Jesus. I think it just came over me that they were saying that everything's going to be okay. That experience told me that I was on my path, and that there were many good things yet to come.

Church, of course, is not the only place of spiritual inspiration. Each of us has our own heritages or traditions that inspire us and facilitate our connection to something larger than we are. Begin to seek out places of worship that touch your heart and draw you. There are many pathways to divine connection. Find yours.

Meditation

Whether you are drawn to houses of worship or not, all of us can find a great source of spiritual sustenance and expansion through meditation.

As powerful as my church experience was, I still didn't feel like I was home. There was still something missing that I couldn't put my finger on. During this time, someone had suggested that meditation would be good for me and that might be where I could find the answers that I was desperately seeking.

I started researching meditations, looking at guided meditations online. I had no idea at the time how powerful and important meditation would be for me as a part of my spiritual journey. It was just an idea that someone had mentioned, and I said "yes."

Meditation allowed me to open my third eye and connect with my higher self. After I'd been meditating for some time, I began to have supernatural experiences that came to me during meditation. Visions, faces, Bible verses, and dreams started coming to me. I was tapping into the supernatural realm. Meditation became a place where my guides and other Spirits who were looking out for me would send me messages.

You, too, can have access to all the benefits of meditation if you do not already engage in a regular meditative practice.

As you progress along your journey of psychic development, begin with a guided meditation every day for two weeks, and then eventually graduate to silent meditation, because you need to be able to quiet the mind to hear the soul. Meditation is such a simple thing, but its effect on you and your life can be monumental and become an important part of your healing journey. If you are sick and tired of being sick and tired, and you feel from the depths of your soul that you were meant to do more—and you just don't know what it is—I encourage you to listen to the guidance within you. And the best way to do this is to quiet the mind.

Meditation is a vehicle for connecting not only to Spirit but to your guides and the unknown. It is also a great way to connect with your soul and discover what your higher self is trying to tell you. Meditation allows you to connect to your body and soul, and the very love within. Every spiritual teacher that I've met along my journey has said, "Meditation is the core. You have to develop a meditative practice, and it must become a discipline." I recommend starting your healing journey right now with meditation, easing into it with guided meditations first.

Each and every one of us is being divinely guided. When you feel that you have had enough of doing things the same old way, that is your "spiritual team" saying that now is the time to seek out these experiences. Whether it be in church, in meditation, or someplace else, you can find opportunities to heal through spiritual avenues.

I started by listening to the guided meditations of medium Gordon Smith on YouTube. There are many people offering guided meditations, but I strongly recommend finding ones that are led by psychic mediums as they have a very particular focus that will help you to develop your abilities.

Every morning, set aside ten to fifteen minutes to get comfortable in a safe space where no one will interrupt you, and allow yourself time to find that quiet inside. Meditation is a full body experience. It makes you feel floaty, and lets you turn off the business of the mind and root yourself into your body. As you progress over time, you'll start to transcend mind and body and connect to something higher. Silence the mind. Hear the soul.

Why do I recommend guided meditations in particular? They offer a kind of support that can be very helpful in the beginning. We all have that monkey mind at first, and I know it is going to fight you on meditating—"I can't do it. I can't do it. I can't do it,"—but you *can* do it. Meditation is a discipline and training—and it is just showing up.

We have to be able to shut down the mind so we can hear Spirit. You can do silent meditations once you've gone through guided meditations. Start learning with your guided meditations to calm down, listen to your body, and be in the moment. Commit the time to do them, and then finally move into a silent meditation where you are sitting in a quiet space just concentrating on your breath and holding the silence.

This can be the hardest thing for most people: to be comfortable in silence, to be completely alone with themselves without even their own thoughts running through their head to distract them, to learn to be completely there in that moment. As Michael Alan Singer, the author of *The Untethered Soul,* explains, "This place of centered awareness is the seat of the witness, the seat of Self. That is the only seat from which you can let go. There is nothing more important to true growth than realizing that you are not the voice of the mind—you are the one who hears it."

I have a technique that I teach in my classes; I call it the *candle technique.* If you are having a hard time shutting off your mind, then close your eyes and visualize a candle in front of you. Imagine the candle burning and keep a single-minded intention to concentrate on the flame. When your mind starts to drift to the grocery list or anywhere else, acknowledge the thought, and come back to the candle. This will train the brain to be quiet, and with practice, it will just go into silence and expand your awareness.

I have had a daily meditative practice for five years now. I suggest to my clients and students that they be disciplined and meditate every single day. After the first month or so, you'll start to feel something different. You will start connecting to a higher power and will reach something deeper inside yourself. Meditation takes discipline and practice—and is well worth it, as you will discover.

Every person's timeframe for learning to quiet the mind will be different, just as their meditation experiences will be. Some people may feel lightheaded or floaty, while others see colors or have visions. You may find you receive messages or thoughts from somewhere outside yourself. Meditation can be a gateway to powerful spiritual or psychic experiences, but there is nothing to fear. Meditation may also heighten your perception throughout the day, and the world could become more vibrant and alive. Many meditators gain greater awareness of colors, dreams, and signs from beyond.

Meditation is key to so many aspects of spiritual development. It can accelerate your healing, and really help you with whatever it is you are looking to accomplish. I recommend meditation both as a way to start your journey, and to further your path wherever you are along it. Meditation really is that powerful.

Journaling

As you start on the next part of your journey, you will become aware of the things in your life that are holding you back: things that have caused you pain, or coping strategies you've learned that aren't serving you anymore. These might include limiting or harmful beliefs. I call these *blocks*. Blocks are the walls that you've built up around yourself and around your heart due to the trauma, hurt, pain, and disappointments—everything in life that has happened to you that has caused you to protect yourself from more trauma.

We don't get to the space in our life where we need healing without putting up walls, and it is difficult to penetrate those walls. To truly heal and incorporate your past into a whole version of yourself, it will be crucial to start breaking down the blocks.

Brick by brick, you need to dismantle the wall that pain built. You need to do this so your heart and soul can open up again, and so you can let the light in and heal yourself. This work is very important to your path; tearing down the wall will further enable you to connect to Spirit, so you can do your work and live your mediumship.

I would like to share an image that has been particularly helpful to me and my clients. It comes from one of my favorite songs, "Another Brick in the Wall" by Pink Floyd. I visualize all my hurts over the years, my letdowns, my traumas, my drug abuse—everything bad that has ever happened to me—as one brick in the wall that I built to shield myself.

The wall was created to keep out the pain; but ultimately, it was shutting out everything. It prevented me from being in touch with my feelings, and it made it impossible for me to experience love and feel alive. Maybe it kept out some darkness, but it also couldn't let in the light.

Picture all your hurt, your letdowns, your traumas—everything painful that's happened to you in your life to this point. Picture every experience as a brick in your wall that needs to be healed. Your healing journey at this point is to start taking every brick down: experiencing it, feeling it, healing it, and letting it go.

To do that, I suggest you start a practice of journaling. Journaling allows you to get your thoughts and feelings out in a productive way; it gives you perspective and allows you to be an observer to your experiences and emotions, rather than merely reacting to them. You can see your life and the people and situations in it from a soul's perspective, instead of from the view of a hurt child and a source of trauma. It allows you to start understanding the lessons your experiences hold. Journaling will be a very, very big part of your journey.

I suggest you purchase a journal and after every meditation, start journaling. As you come out of your meditation, just pick up your journal and start writing—without thinking, worrying about structure, without caring if anyone sees it—just write. What does your soul need you to hear? I call it *automatic writing*; it is what's coming from deep within you, because you're not thinking about what to write. You're just experiencing it in the moment. You don't have to understand every part of the text; you just need to let yourself express the words as part of your healing process. Just let them come, express, release, and write them down on the page.

As you journal, write about the painful episodes in your lifetime. Go back from birth through the present day. Feel every piece of pain that you've ever felt, then start the healing process in this way:

1. Revisit the incidents without being in them. That is, imagine you are looking down at what is happening as if from a God's-eye view. Let yourself feel compassion for who you were at that time and how you were hurt. Feel the love, the concern, but let go of any victim story. As you look down with a God's-eye view, write down what might have been the lessons of each occurrence. How did each painful moment create your gifts or the blessings of your life?

2. For each incident, write the sentence: "I am not the victim here because . . . ." and explore ways of reframing so that you no longer see yourself as a victim. This does not mean you should

not have compassion or love for your younger self. It is very important that you do.

3. You might even want to write to your younger self, letting him/her know how sorry you are that those things happened, and ask what you can do now to heal and honor the wounded younger self.

4. Explore through describing what took place, have conversations with your past self, and do not censor anything. You may be surprised by some of the wise voices that emerge, and the insights into why each incident was necessary for your soul growth and to become the precious person you are today.

It is natural to not want to revisit difficult events again. It can feel as if you are opening wounds by touching them, but if you want to take away the pain from them completely, you need to return with new perspective and faith in the larger purpose. Indeed, we need to *feel it to heal it*. There may be some things in your past that are so challenging that you may not be able to work through them alone. If that is the case, please seek professional help. Not everyone can afford to do so, but if you can, it will be an investment in you and your future clients. If you are unable to, explore the past in small steps. There is no need to do things quickly, so stay focused on caring for and nurturing your younger self.

Michael, of *The Untethered Soul*, explains emotional and mental healing is when we can let go of the things in life that are holding us back. These things can be incidents from our childhood, regrets and relationships in the past, and things that we would rather not recall, yet our minds keep turning them over and over, forcing us to recall and relive painful situations.

Below are some sentence starters that might make the process easier for you:

1) Because of my past traumas, I am fearful of_____.

2) I have the following emotions:

a._____

b._____

c._____

d._____

e._____regarding this situation_____.

3) I need to let go of_____. I have no control over it.

4) I need to forgive._____

I need to forgive them/it because_____.

5) The following things trigger me:

a._____

b._____

c._____

d._____

e._____

6) They trigger me because_____.

7) What is no longer serving me?_____.

8) Ways I want to begin healing:_____.

9) If I had to name one emotion that seems to live deep in my core, it would be:_____.

10) What makes me feel safe?_____.

Journaling is a great way to see and experience the painful events that happened to you in a safe way. You can more clearly perceive how the events affected you and start to understand them from a higher perspective. You might even understand the pain that the people who hurt you were in, or the pain they experienced themselves which led them to treat you the way they did. When you're journaling, you want to touch on every aspect of your trauma, from childhood to present, and just address every single thing. You're going to have to *feel it to heal it* in this stage of your journey. Forgive those who need to be forgiven. Understand those who need to be understood. Again, this isn't about them; it's merely about you releasing things from the confines of your brain and heart through the act of writing. You can take the pages and burn them later, if that's what you need to do for your healing. It's just so important to address every aspect of your life and your trauma as you progress. Enjoy the peace that comes from healing the wounds inside yourself. You deserve it.

Your journaling also offers a great way to learn to more fully love yourself. I recommend to everyone who starts journaling to expand the practice to include affirmations and gratitude. When you have experienced significant trauma over the span of a lifetime, your mind tends to focus on the negative and will internalize damaging beliefs. By practicing gratitude and using affirmations, you are starting to train your mind to see the good in yourself and your life. You will also be acknowledging your worth and be more aware of the blessings you have received.

Loving Affirmations and Gratitude

Writing down affirmations every single day is an important part of your healing, as is noting all the things you are grateful for on a daily basis. Begin every day by listing five things that you love about yourself. Then list five things that you are grateful for. You've taken all these years to create the story that you tell yourself, based on the traumas, hurts, pains, and disappointments. It's going to take some time to retrain your brain to think differently.

Focus in the next several months on retraining your mind, body, and soul. You're working on the mind right now. You've got to reassess how you think of yourself and the stories you hold onto. You can do that through journaling, practicing gratitude, doing affirmations, and learning to love your true, authentic self.

During the personal healing part of my psychic mediumship development, I journaled every morning, after meditation, and sometimes even at night before I went to bed. Journaling at the end of the day helps to address feelings and triggers experienced. Write about the people who have hurt you, really going deep and feeling it so you can heal. Get mad, get sad, cry. This stage of your healing is not easy, but it is necessary. Resentment, guilt, criticism, and a victim mentality can be like a cancer to your mental state and your body. Break through those chains that bind you to an unhappy, unhealthy life and past. You can give yourself the gift of freedom, so you can build a stronger, happier, healthier foundation for your future and your mediumship going forward.

Overcoming Triggers

Being triggered means that something someone does or says affects you in a negative way, and you tend to lash out or seek to escape. When that happens, your traumas come into play and become projected onto other people. Frequently, others have no intention to hurt you. However, your reactions become over the top, because what they said triggered something within you. Maybe it brought out the time in your past when someone told you that you weren't good enough, or you weren't lovable or beautiful. Someone hurt you. Sometimes people's actions can affect you in that way—you get triggered and overreact or become impulsive.

In the beginning of your healing, you will likely experience triggers and reactions, instead of having control. Journaling every night about how your day went and what triggered you can help you to recognize what those triggers are, and to notice how you react to them. Journaling can help you figure out how you'd prefer to respond and can help you find strategies that work for you to accomplish that. Hopefully, through healing, you'll stop being reactive and just exist in a state of peace and well-being. That would enable you to react with equanimity in those cases when someone actually intends to hurt you.

I think the first step—recognizing that you're being triggered—indicates an awareness of self. To be able to see clearly what is happening and how it is affecting you, and how you're reacting to it, is *awareness*. You can sense when you're about to be triggered, because your emotions start to intensify, and you feel something building inside. It is that feeling that we are attaching a negative emotion to—the feeling that's rising up that was "caused" by somebody else.

The first step to healing is acknowledging when you are triggered. Breathe through it. Count to ten before you react. Step away from the situation, or from the computer if you are challenged by a specific email or video. Allow yourself a few minutes to get out of the space of reaction based on feeling, and instead, logically dissect what happened.

Walk through it in your mind like you would talk to a friend: What did the person say? Do you think it was meant the way you took it? Was the intention to hurt you? What else might they have meant? Why does it feel so painful to you?

Then talk yourself through your reaction to it and how you would like to react to this situation in the future. You can give yourself a strategy for the next time: Perhaps you will breathe slowly and count to ten. Perhaps you will recite a few words that speak to you and remind you of your worth, of your journey, and the progress you've made. Some examples could be affirmations like these:

"I am so much stronger now."

"I am a beacon of love and that starts with me."

"No one can make me feel inferior without my permission."

"I can choose to respond with strength and love."

Remember, this is soul work, but it is also mind work. Our brain learned to respond to these triggers with fear and anger, and we are teaching it another way. Working with your triggers is similar to meditating: when your mind wanders, gently pull it back to your practice. When your mind starts to react and you feel your emotional response escalate, gently pull it back, guiding your mind towards calmness and love.

Being reactive is not being fair and authentic to your own true self. It is like playing a part in a script you don't need anymore—experiencing pain, fear, or anger when it is not necessary. You can learn to move past those old roles, to feel and respond to what's happening now in your life and not relive old stories over and over again. You are empowered to step away from situations and calm your feelings down, so that you are not reacting emotionally, but with logic. Then you can go back to the other person and say, "Hey, this is why I was triggered."

You won't be reacting with emotion and anger, because you've had time to process it. That allows you to come to the table with healthy dialogue. That's the difference. Most people stay in a reactive space, and that's where it becomes toxic, because you're projecting onto the other person. They naturally become defensive because harm was not their intent. However, if you can step back and count to ten, take the emotions out of your response, and come around to a logical way of thinking, you can quickly defuse the situation. Understand why you were triggered and then explain it to them this way: "This is what you said, and because of my past, this is what I heard, and this is how I responded." You can start to build trust with them and improve your communication and relationship. It is definitely something that you can work through, and if it involves someone you love in your life, that person may be able to help you by doing or saying things differently.

A personal example is that my boyfriend enjoys alcohol, and he has given me gifts of alcohol. There have been no indications that alcohol is a problem for him and has in no way affected me or him negatively. However, alcohol is a trigger for me because of the negative role it played in my childhood. The first time he gifted me a bottle of beautiful vintage wine, I felt prickly and unappreciative. I witnessed my own response and realized right away that my reaction was about the past, not my boyfriend's current kindness. By recognizing when we are responding to old traumas, we live with choice and create fewer unnecessary conflicts and dramas for ourselves and those we love.

In the evening, pull out your journal and ask yourself, "Well, what triggered me, and why did it trigger me?" Get to the root of the problem. The other person may have said something ugly, but why allow that to affect your emotions? If we love ourselves and we are confident within ourselves, the things that others say just don't affect us that strongly. So, what part of us thought that their comment may have had some truth to it to the point where we got angry?

At the same time, if there are people in your life who are saying and doing hurtful things—injuring you, your self-confidence, and your self-worth—you need to recognize and respond to that as well. Being triggered happens when something that shouldn't really hurt you causes you to feel or respond as you did when things were truly damaging. However, there are times people do intentionally say things to hurt us.

You deserve love and respect and that can mean deciding what relationships are good for you and your growth and limiting your contact with people who aren't. That's where journaling comes in again—to really get authentic and deep with yourself. We have to figure out what the reaction is about, so that we can gauge our responses appropriately.

The only person in life you can ever control is yourself. You can't control how others treat you or talk to you, but you can control your reactions and how you let them affect you. That control only comes, however, when your worthiness reflects your ability to allow your feelings to matter. This healing is part of our soul work. We must reach deep and choose how we want to respond to triggers, how we recognize them and, ultimately, how we let them go. Your past is not your present, and today you can actively choose a more vibrant and loving future.

Learning to Love Yourself

The next stage on your journey is learning to love yourself. This is probably one of the most important things you will work on throughout your healing journey. If you don't love yourself, then how will others be able to love you the way you need to be loved?

It's going to take considerable time to retrain your thinking; have patience and give yourself grace. Remember, lack of self-worth is another expression of lack of self-love. Catch yourself any time you start to talk negatively about yourself and turn it into a positive. Acknowledge your worth and appreciate your gifts, your Spirit, and your ability to love.

You are starting to learn to retrain your brain to think positively. This is where living in a constant state of gratitude becomes important. List in your journal every day five things you're grateful for. Start off every day in a place of gratitude. For instance, "I'm just grateful I woke up today," can be a powerful way to start your day. And then, "I love this about myself." If you start every day with five things that you're grateful for and five things that you love about yourself, then you've started the day in a mindset that is positive. And if you can, just keep that positive space throughout the entire day; you have then gained another day towards happiness.

We are all human and there will be some bad days. There will be days you forget to journal. There will be days you are not grateful for anything. And on those days especially, I want you to give yourself grace. Grace is a thing that you probably haven't thought about giving yourself in the past, but if you need permission, I'll give it to you. *Give yourself grace on the bad days.* All we can do is start the very next day over again, and be okay that we had a bad day, because we are human. We're going to have bad days. The key is to step it back up the next day and try again, and never give up, and just keep on trying. I promise you that the bad days will start to diminish.

Let's go deeper into gratitude. Our lives are about mind, body, soul, and how we pull them together, how we think about things and understand them, how we take care of our bodies and experience them, and how we touch Spirit and welcome it into our lives. Gratitude is about the mind. The mind is a very powerful tool, and you'll become even more aware on your mediumship journey just how powerful the mind is. Our thoughts create our reality, so if you are in a place of negativity all the time, you are going to create a negative space for your life. Like attracts like, so then you'll start to notice more negative things in your life. Your car will break down, things will go wrong, and you'll never have enough. These are the types of experiences that you're going to attract. Learning to practice gratitude changes your vibration. If you can practice gratitude in everything you do, you're naturally raising your vibration.

When you have a higher vibration, you create a different reality. That's what gratitude creates—a different way of looking at life: instead of it happening **to** *you*, it is happening **for** *you*.

Gratitude is one of the most important tools in your spiritual healing toolbox right from the beginning because it will literally change your outlook on life. If we are happy and we are in a place of gratitude, we're going to start attaining better things in our lives

Last, learn to use affirmations. Just as thoughts can contribute to a negative reality, they can also create a positive reality. You get to choose the reality in which you live. Using affirmations will help you to create a positive reality by stating positive things about yourself and your life as if they were facts.

The more you say it, the more your brain believes it. Affirmations can be as simple as: "I am beautiful," "I am loving," or "I am abundant." They can be anything that you are currently trying to focus on during your healing. My favorite affirmation during my journey was, "You are meant to be greater than you are." I knew that I was meant for a greater purpose. At the time, I had not recognized exactly what that was yet, but my soul knew. The soul always knows.

Affirmations are a powerful tool to combat negative mental habits we've learned. We have to train our brain to believe the things we're telling it now, because this is a new concept for our mind. Gratitude is a new concept for us. Loving ourselves is too, at this point in our healing journey. Affirmations help to reinforce the new story that you are now telling your brain. I sometimes write my affirmations on the bathroom mirror because I need to be reminded frequently: "I am good enough. I am meant to be better than I am." I wrote this affirmation all over the place. I wrote it on sticky notes and left them wherever I could.

Affirmations are positive statements that have two purposes: first, they help overcome self-sabotaging negative thoughts, and second, they can be used as statements of fact so that the intention is put out into the Universe. It's all about energy and vibration. Speak what you desire into existence.

To use affirmations, first analyze the thoughts or behaviors that you'd like to change in your life. For example, if you are having a hard time loving yourself, then create affirmations towards loving yourself such as, "I am love and I am lovable," or "I am worthy of loving myself." I personally use, "I love myself more than anyone else matters," because I always put other people first. More examples are, "I am meant to be greater than I am," "I am loving," "I am kind," or "I am beautiful." If you are struggling with a financial situation, I would create affirmations towards abundance: "I am abundant," "Money comes to me easily," or "I am magnetic to health, wealth, abundance, and prosperity."

Here are some other examples. Feel free to use some or all of them for your daily affirmations.

Money

I attract money effortlessly.

Wealth flows easily into my life.

I am a money magnet.

I release all resistance to attracting money.

Money is energy and it flows into my life constantly.

Money is pouring into my life.

I breathe abundance.

Love/Romance

I give my heart and am ready to receive the heart of another.

I am making room for an amazing partner in my life.

I deserve love and affection.

I am attracting the perfect person for me.

I am in the healthiest relationship of my life.

I am open to love.

I am prepared to receive love.

I naturally find love everywhere.

Job

I have my dream job.

I have limitless potential.

I am open to new opportunities.

I am confident.

I am an asset.

Tell yourself you are enough, lovable, loved; tell yourself you are meant to be greater than you are—affirm all these things. Start by writing ten affirmations about yourself to get started in the process, and then live by those affirmations. How about taking a minute right now to list five, just to get you going and give you some hands-on practice?

Here is part two of the above practice: Sit in front of a mirror. Stare into your own eyes (eyes are the windows to the soul), and state five affirmations about yourself. State them as if they are facts. Keep looking into your eyes every time. Repeat.

Read your affirmations every single day—and if it helps, include the mirror exercise above. Post your affirmations everywhere that you can so that you start to believe them because that's the key. Retrain the brain to believe a different story. You may start out thinking that these positive new beliefs aren't true. You may think that you know better, but that's your past talking: that's your trauma and your pain talking. You are a human being; you were created for this time and this journey. You are part of God and the Universe made manifest in a body. You are a soul experiencing this life. You are beautiful, you are strong and good, worthy of love, and you are loved.

Think of those people you love or loved completely in your life, such as a parent or grandparent, a child, a sibling, or a friend. Imagine them struggling with the same feelings, insecurities, or limiting beliefs that you feel. Feel in your heart how strongly you would rise up to their defense, how deeply you *know* that they are wonderful and deserving of every good thing in this life, regardless of what they think or feel, regardless of what may have happened to them, or what they have done. Hold onto that feeling, that passion and love and certainty, because you are deserving of it as well. It is what the Universe and your guides and everyone that has loved you would feel and say in your defense. It is what I am telling you now.

Practice affirmations and self-love not because you *want* those things to be true, but practice them because they *are* true, and you are reclaiming them. You are teaching your mind to accept the truth after it has been hurt, or lied to, or you've lost belief in yourself. You can learn to believe in yourself, in the good in you, and the good you are capable of. In doing so, you can start to live more, love more, and give more.

As you begin to recreate your narrative, you will begin to fully realize these wise words from *The Untethered Soul*, by Michael Alan Singer: "You will not be able to solve anything on the outside until you own how the situation affects you on the inside."

Inspiration and Self-Expression

Along your healing journey, it's very important to feed the mind, raise your sights and thoughts to greater things, and open up to wonderful possibilities. We keep talking about the mind, because the mind is such a powerful thing in our spiritual journey. Our minds contain so much of our trauma, our memories, and experiences that hold the negative beliefs or destructive patterns that we're trying to heal.

Many of us have experienced so much trauma that it's vital that we nourish our minds with positive information. During your healing journey process, I recommend reading self-help books. Reading a good book is like being in the room with a teacher, sitting with an inspirational friend, or being guided by the wisest person you know.

There are three books that jumpstarted my journey. The very first book was *The Secret* by Rhonda Byrne; then, *The Untethered Soul* by Michael Alan Singer; and last, *The Four Agreements* by Don Miguel Ruiz. You won't agree with everything, but if you have an open mind, you'll find things that will inspire you to take the next step on your path.

Another inspiration in my healing journey was the work of Esther Hicks. Esther Hicks channels a collective called Abraham. A collective is a group of entities in Spirit that share a common issue or interest or work together to achieve a common objective. Her teachings were simple, yet life-changing for me. Esther Hicks is brilliant at how she helps people see just how simple it is supposed to be. Listening to her videos every morning, while getting ready for work, set my attitude into a state of gratitude. She says that our job here on this planet is to be happy and to seek unconditional love. With all the need and trauma I had experienced, her teachings were a revelation. My job was to be happy and seek love; it is so simple. We humans make this life super-complicated, but really, it is not as complicated as we make it out to be. We are souls having a human experience, and we are here to learn lessons.

Self-expression is a great tool for inner healing. Creative acts help process pain, ignite interests and passions, unlock your inner child, and boost your curiosity. Painting became very therapeutic for me, as I could channel my inner Van Gogh. Painting, drawing, and writing music are all ways that you can go deep within to express feelings and emotions. You can find whatever artistic medium or media that speaks to you, whether poetry, sewing clothes, or woodworking. If you feel drawn to something and it allows for creative self-expression, give yourself permission to explore it. Eventually, you'll find something that is a satisfying vehicle for you. Self-expression is also a form of vulnerability as you reveal yourself through your creation. You don't have to share the results; lean into the act of creation as a healing act, a form of self-discovery. Let yourself be as free as you wish. Leave all judgments, including your own, behind.

Adding this type of creativity and imagination to your life will also help your psychic development. Medium Lisa Williams taught me that imagination has a direct correlation to mediumship. One of my most "Aha!" moments in my mediumship journey came from Lisa Williams during a workshop I was taking. She taught me about the distinct functions of the brain.

There are two hemispheres of the brain, and each relates to very different ways of processing—the left brain, which is activated when we are thinking analytically, and the right brain, which is engaged when we are involved in more creative and even spiritual pursuits. Williams explained that Spirit talks to us via the right brain in more intuitive and metaphoric ways, while the left brain, being analytical, often discounts the information that appears less rational and literal.

To be a successful medium, it is critical to become aware of the very different ways each brain hemisphere relates to and processes information. Meditation aids in our ability to identify and access the right brain, which is less verbal, more feeling-based and metaphoric. This is also why being creative is so important. When you are able to quiet the left brain that is associated with rational, critical thought, and can cultivate your ability to see and think in ways that involve color, feeling, and gestalts, you can better communicate with the afterlife. The better you can open your brain to imagination, the more effective your storytelling will be and the more "wow" evidence you'll receive. Mediumship is very right-brain focused, so nurture your creativity, your imagination, and self-expression.

We all have this little creative side to us; however, we become so busy in life that we don't listen to or nurture that creative side of us. We don't do things that make us happy and creative, because we're just trying to work, survive, marry, and have children, and our creativity has been stifled. My prayer for you is that your creativity be reborn. Return to doing things that you love to do. And even if you've never done it, try it. I did it with painting; I bought dozens of brushes, canvases, and tubes of paint. I locked myself in a room, and just allowed myself to explore. Find the thing that resonates with you. It could be cooking, gardening, writing, scrapbooking, to name just a few. The key is to let your imagination flow.

Roadmap through the Healing Process

To begin your healing journey, this is what I suggest—and is the roadmap I followed to become The Red Couch Medium. Feel free to adjust based on your own needs.

- Walk for twenty minutes in nature every day.
- Meditate for twenty minutes every day.
- Journal for twenty minutes every day.
   *In your journal, write down five things you are grateful for and five things that you love about yourself.
- Listen to Esther Hicks, one video every day.
- Heal your past traumas; journal them; turn anything negative into a positive.
- Use affirmations and quotes.
- Love yourself more than anyone else matters.

When you embark on a spiritual journey and begin developing your mediumship, by going within and delving deeply into emotion, you inherently create an environment for your own healing. Mediumship and mending run side by side. A teacher once told me, "Whatever is wrong with your mediumship is what is wrong in your life, or what has been left unhealed." When I began my journey, I lacked trust and confidence. I had to heal the areas of my life that caused me to be distrustful and lose confidence in myself. I had to heal those wounds so I could bring my whole spirit to my work. I had to understand, accept, and forgive. I had to no longer allow those negative emotions to rule my mind.

Your mind is so powerful, and mediumship is all in the mind. When you heal yourself, you will not only find it possible to go deeper into your mediumship, to connect more completely with Spirit, but you will allow yourself peace and happiness in all areas of your life. Don't underestimate how important this is. As a medium, you are acting as the connection to the Spirit world. All communication and information come through you. Even if you don't yet see how deeply you deserve healing, know that healing will deepen and strengthen what you receive and can communicate. The calling of mediumship is a call to positive transformation, to nurture and love yourself, so that you can offer uplifting transformation to others.

Dr. Nicole LePera, The Holistic Psychologist and author of *How to Do the Work: Recognize Your Patterns, Heal from Your Past, and Create Your Self*, states that there are five stages of healing:

Stage one: shock, shame, and despair. This phase represents the beginning of awakening to the conditioned self, an understanding of our own patterns and behaviors that changes life as we know it. Facing ourselves is confronting and can bring up challenging emotions.

Stage two: hope and deeper awareness. The next step is having a belief that life can hold deeper meaning, that we are more than our conditioned, autopilot self. With new awareness, we become conscious of how our choices create our reality.

Stage three: grief. As we process childhood trauma, limiting beliefs, and understand our coping mechanisms, we grieve for the former version of ourselves. We also mourn for our inner child that felt misunderstood, unseen, or unheard. On a deeper level, we may also feel grief for the entire traumatized collective.

Stage four: acceptance and self-awareness. As we go along our journey, we begin to slowly surrender and accept all parts of ourselves. We have a greater understanding of ourselves and who we actually are, which allows us to show up from a space of vulnerability, compassion, and grace.

And then, the final stage of healing: living the purpose-driven life. Life no longer becomes about external success or appearance. We crave deeper, more authentic connections to others; we seek to serve, give, and value community. Our own liberation inspires others to liberate themselves. Period.

I didn't initially set out to be a medium. It was through healing my traumas that my passion for mediumship naturally happened. From the other side of my healing, I am living the most joyful life I've ever lived. I am experiencing peace I never had before. I am free of the fear and numbness and pain that defined so much of my life. I can connect to the people I love and can love them un-conditionally. No one is making me happy. Money is not making me happy. Things are not making me happy. My soul is happy and finally at peace.

Healing is a choice. It is the biggest step towards inner happi-ness and peace you will ever take. No one can tell you when the time is right or how to do it. It is knowing that will come deep from within your soul. Know that you can heal and that you deserve to heal. Know that living a life full of love and self-acceptance is not a selfish act, but rather one that allows you to give love, support, and healing to others. Know that the Universe wants you to become the happiest and most fulfilled version of yourself because that is where you will do the most good in this world. I know the journey can be long, and healing can bring its own pain as you address your traumas, but I know that you can—and it's the most impor-tant thing you will ever do.

CHAPTER THREE

THE RED COUCH

Every relationship has a spiritual purpose that helps us grow and become stronger. Sometimes, our most challenging relationships bring the greatest personal blessings. From them we learn about forgiveness, patience, and other virtues.

-Doreen Virtue

One cold winter day, my boyfriend and I decided to go for a hike in the Plano area. There were lovely, wooded areas with hiking trails in the area we lived in. A cool mist hung above the brown grasses. We walked for a long while, and my eye was drawn to the red in the veins of the few leaves remaining on the trees. I saw a group of cardinals brightly contrasted against the low-hanging clouds. Brilliant red—I sensed that it was a sign. These red birds were a sign from beyond as clearly as if my father were right there beside me.

I was finally aware of what it was like to have an experience with the afterworld. I was finally starting to see signs and understand messages. I had missed them all those years, but now it was as though I could see them for the first time. I was connecting my soul to these experiences and it had become overwhelmingly exciting for me. I knew the birds were a sign—I could feel my father's presence in them. But there was something more. As we started hiking back, I stopped mid-trail and looked at my boyfriend and said, "How random would it be if there was a red couch out here in the middle of nowhere?"

Because he knew I was going through a lot of changes, he didn't tell me that I was crazy, but he said, "That's kind of a weird thought." I knew it wasn't, and I didn't know where the thought came from, but I just had to say it.

We ended that hike and went on with our day, never seeing a red couch. Still, the color of red was popping up everywhere for me. There was something more to the message that I hadn't seen yet.

A week later, my clothes dryer broke. I had teenagers and college-aged kids living at the house at the time, so having the dryer break created a hardship. I had to take the wet, washed clothes down to the laundromat. My boyfriend volunteered to hang out with me, so we met up there. I put everything in the dryer, and we let it run. It was a Saturday morning so it was crowded, and I just hated being there. My boyfriend said, "How about we just go take a walk?" It was an early morning in February, so it was cold outside, but we both were longing for some fresh air.

Right behind the laundromat was a big, open field and then a lake. As we started walking, I took his hand as we strolled down the path. We crossed to the back of the building, and as soon as we hit the open field, he froze, a look of shock on his face. I asked what the matter was, and he pointed. There in the middle of this field of wheat-gold grass was an abandoned red couch. I was so flabbergasted that I couldn't believe what I saw, but at the same time, it was as if I knew this moment was coming. I felt as if the couch itself was speaking to me in a symbolic language. I was being nudged by my dad, and the Spirit world, to follow this emerging desire I had. The red couch was an affirmation that I was to become a medium.

I don't know how I knew that my father was orchestrating all of this. He was the one helping me get me to the point I needed to be, through all the tragedy that I had suffered. The moment I saw the red couch, I felt it validated all my affirmations that something greater awaited me than the life I was living. The Spirit world, and everything else around me, was foreshadowing what was yet to come. Spirit's message was simple: Open your eyes. It is all around you. You are being called.

At this period in my life, when I first saw this red couch as a symbol, as part of my journey, is when synchronicities were introduced to me. I learned that Spirit speaks through synchronicities. I learned about the idea of sacred coincidences, and suddenly they revealed themselves everywhere. I learned that Spirit speaks through synchronicity and symbols, like the color red showing up everywhere, like the cardinals. I had never seen a red bird in my life, and suddenly, I was seeing red birds everywhere. They may have been there the whole time, but in my state of awareness, I never recognized them or knew them. They didn't mean anything to me before then. Synchronicities became very relevant to me, and to my state of awareness. Through my healing and journaling, there came an awareness around me of people and places and things, and of how synchronicity works.

I also came to learn through the spiritual community that cardinals are little messengers from Heaven. If this was a message, what else might be? How does Spirit talk? I became more curious to explore how Spirit communicates with us. I always thought they would show up in my bedroom as full-on ghosts, speaking to me. That's just not how it works. So many people don't realize the many ways we can receive messages from the other side, and they miss the opportunity to realize the magic that's there. We can't experience signs and symbols if we don't know how to look for them. If you're waiting to receive a letter, you might miss a song playing over and over on the radio. You may be waiting for a ghost, and you've been sent a rainbow. We must learn to look for the messages all around us so we can see what they are telling us. Who would have ever thought a red couch would be one of the ways Spirit, especially my dad, would connect with me?

I was finally being made aware of how Spirit speaks, and I was making that connection. I was living in a place of total awareness about myself and my surroundings. My mind had opened up at this point. I was seeing, hearing, and feeling Spirit all around me. I was opening up to the world, and to experiences, and I was receiving messages and signs in so many different ways. I was seeing the world anew and witnessing the work of Spirit everywhere. I was ready to become a medium.

As you are journaling, I want you to start a list of any synchronicities that you notice. Start looking for the things that are showing up repeatedly, like numbers or colors—things that you are encountering over and over. Any of these could be a message from a loved one on the other side or from Spirit. Besides visual messages, you can have audio messages as well. I would hear my name being called. I'd be all alone in the house, and I would literally hear my name being called. I knew that it was my dad. I just knew it. These communications can be audible or high-pitched sounds in the ear. You might notice the same song playing on the radio numerous times. I sometimes feel tingles when Spirit is connecting to me.

The key is beginning to unlock Spirit communication. This process begins through journaling the things that you notice, and being open to all the sounds, feelings, symbols, and senses that fill your days.

The red couch was a powerful symbol for me throughout my journey of developing my psychic and mediumistic skills and has appeared in all kinds of places over the years. When I trained for the first time with Colby Rebel in Los Angeles, I was walking from my hotel to her spiritual center. There, across the street, in clear view, sat an abandoned red couch. During a healing trip to Belize, I spotted another discarded red couch on a pier. That's how Spirit encourages us. The red couches that I see along my journey validate that I am on the right path. They were all abandoned, a little funky and tattered; velvet, tweed, and Victorian style—and all abandoned. Every time I see one now, I know I am on the right path. I am good.

One spring evening, as I was settling into sleep, between dream and wakefulness, I remembered a memory that had been locked away for years. I saw myself at nineteen, in my bedroom, holding a tear-soaked white tissue in my hand and crying. I was preparing to dress for my father's funeral. I looked at my closet filled with clothes, knowing that the right thing to do would be to wear black. But something in me had the desire to make my own mark—one that would be full of life, energy, and passion. I reached for a bright red dress to honor my father that day. I had totally forgotten about this incident until that one evening decades later.

I felt goosebumps on my arms and neck as I was recalling this memory. Then it all became clear: my father, on the other side, must have witnessed me at his funeral in that daring crimson dress, and for all the years that followed, he would let me know that he saw me in red on that day.

When I realized that connection, I felt an even greater knowing that it was my calling to be a medium. I know that my father remains with me on every step of my journey, as do the red couches that appear to remind me that I am, at last, doing the work that I was meant to do.

What might be the signs in your life that are appearing—your version of a red couch? Spirit talks to us and appears to us in so many ways. It can be blinding, but it can also be subtle. It can be hearing a loved one's favorite song, seeing their face in a crowd, or a long-forgotten memory that comes back to you. We rush through life and often miss not only the beauty around us, but the messages as well. Allow yourself to see, hear, and feel the moments of your life. Pay attention to the little things, to the color of houses, and the signs in shop windows. Savor birds singing, music, sunsets, and Christmas lights. Enjoy summer ice cream and Thanksgiving pie. Stop and smell roses or honeysuckle and remember when you smelled them last. Remember those you've loved. Keep your eyes, ears, and heart open to all the synchronicities around you; the symbols may, indeed, be messages from Spirit.

CHAPTER FOUR

ASK AND YOU SHALL RECEIVE

Don't try to steer the river.
-Deepak Chopra

At this point of my journey, Spirit started to leave me other "breadcrumbs" besides red couches. Every choice I made, every new person that I encountered, would have a meaning and purpose. I wouldn't realize this until much later in my journey, but looking back in retrospect, I can now see everything was part of a master plan.

My First Exposure to Mediums

In October of 2012, I happened to come across an ad for a Halloween Mediumship Gallery event in Dallas. It was a unique event as it featured six different mediums, instead of the customary one. At this point in my journey, I had no idea that mediums were everywhere. I was stunned that this was something that would be offered locally. I literally thought that the only mediums out there were the celebrity mediums who had television shows and had written books.

Because I had never been to a medium before, I was excited to attend the gallery, not knowing what to expect. I had only seen television shows or talk shows with mediums on them as guests. There were maybe fifty or sixty people in the small room of the convention center. I went in with the hope of hearing from a loved one, but just being in the presence of six mediums, and the possibilities of what could happen, really excited me.

As the mediums came on stage, my attention was drawn to two specific people. The first was Jennifer Farmer. She was wearing a pair of beautiful blue butterfly wings that gently swayed to fairy music as she bounced down the aisle. She made a distinct impression on me with her wings and her light, airy mood. I now understand that butterflies are part of her branding, but since this was the very first experience I'd ever had with any medium, I was so intrigued, almost shocked, at her presenting herself that way.

The second one who drew me in was "The Cowboy Psychic," Steve Spur. He had a matter-of-fact style. He told the story about how he had been a skeptic. He never believed in any of "this stuff." He had, indeed, been a cowboy. He thought there was no way that there could be anything in the afterworld. His belief system had been that we're here and then we're gone. Then one day, he fell from the attic after suffering a heat stroke, and he suffered a major brain injury. That one event changed his life. After his accident, he started seeing and hearing things. He really thought he was going crazy, until he finally came to the realization that he was connecting with people on the other side. The injury that occurred during that fall triggered something in his brain. He brought through people in Spirit for the audience and provided detailed evidence about each person. It was really fascinating to watch, especially for someone who had not had an experience of afterlife contact yet.

Jennifer Farmer, on the other hand, didn't tell her story. She was a gifted entertainer, however. Where Steve Spur just sat on his stool and spoke matter-of-factly, Jennifer brought animation, entertainment, and joy for a lot of people in the room through her presence and presentation.

Their styles were similar, though, in the sense that they both brought through evidence of past memories to people in the audience. The mediums were very similar in style, but very different in presentation. Mediums can reach people in different ways and people will respond differently to different aspects. Someone more skeptical might feel more at ease with someone who shared their skepticism, while someone more drawn to magic might feel pulled to fairy wings and effervescence. Presentation is part of a medium's outreach, their signature, and their brand so that they are memorable, but fairy wings are not enough. What matters most is the evidence—the memories and messages that come through via Spirit. Jennifer Farmer and Steve Spur were both talented psychic mediums who offered people wonderful connections to the other side.

A gallery reading is an opportunity to watch mediums demonstrate their abilities in an audience setting. Usually, a gallery event is less expensive than an individual reading, so more people will often attend in the hope that they'll get a message without having to pay more.

The unique thing about a gallery event is that even if you don't get a message personally, the messages for other people will sometimes hit home and create healing in itself. I remember being in the gallery and, even though I didn't get a message, hearing my grandmother's name called out for somebody else created its own healing. Hearing other messages that hit home for people, seeing people hear proof of the afterlife, and finding peace and happiness with some of the experiences they had, created healing and magic for me. It was a powerful experience to witness, to be part of. Even if there is not a direct message for you at a gallery event, being in the presence of the healing of other people becomes healing in itself.

I learned so much that day about how mediums work, how widespread their audiences were, and the comforting effects of receiving communication from Spirit. That first gallery event was wonderful and left me wanting more. It brought me closer to what I needed, and to where I was going. I still didn't think of mediumship as something I could do; I needed time before I would be ready to become a medium myself. I was still looking for permission to follow my passion for Spirit, but I was getting closer on my journey and was eager to take the next step.

My First Reading

I was so excited by the experience of seeing mediums in person, of feeling the power of Spirit and healing in the room, that I decided to have a reading of my own a few months later. I kept thinking of the joy and happiness that seemed to radiate from Jennifer Farmer, so I chose her for my reading. At that time, a private reading with someone as well-known as she was a lot of money for me—three hundred dollars. But I pushed forward and booked an hour reading from her.

I ended up driving to Hurst, Texas, where Jennifer had an office and did readings. I was so anxious that she would not be able to connect with any of my loved ones, and the money and the trip would be for nothing. I was also worried about what *would* come through if I got a message. My journey through life has not always been a pretty one, with so many private, traumatizing experiences. I was concerned about what my father and grandmother had to say; just knowing that they knew everything I'd been through was scary.

Spirits don't judge us like people do as we react to our own fears and traumas, but I still felt vulnerable. I felt as if I was going on a trip to see them for the first time in a long time and I didn't know what to expect. I wanted them to be proud, or at least to understand that I had done my best. I was very excited and worried, but my reading with Jennifer turned out to be much more than I had expected!

Jennifer is a fairly tall, slender woman with fair skin and curly red hair. She has this beautiful smile, and a kind and lovely demeanor about her—angelic, even without her butterfly wings. She came dressed in business casual, with slacks and a sweater. It was different than I had seen on the stage at the gallery, but still beautiful, nonetheless.

She began by sitting down, and she gave her opening statement, describing how she connects with people on the other side. She started to talk about my dad right away; the majority of the reading was about him. She said she knew that I had lost my father at a fairly young age, and that my father was telling me that it's okay to be angry with him sometimes; that's what fathers are for. Before his death, we had a lot of mending to do from his alcoholism. My experience of the afterlife is that Spirits come through to heal themselves, as well as to deliver messages. They come through to make amends, offer their apologies, and talk about the things that maybe they had done wrong.

It was beautiful to have the chance to talk to my father again. I knew she had connected with him when she described him as a "man who never met a stranger . . . and made friends with everybody," was in the military, and enjoyed his beer—maybe a little *too* much. For so many years, I had been waiting for a message from my father because we had so much left unresolved. I knew that even all our fights and all my teenage drama didn't affect the love and connection we shared. Even knowing that something is true, it's still different to experience it, to have a loved one's presence confirmed, to know my father was in the room with me. I was able to let so much go once I heard from him. Sometimes, when you lose someone—especially someone close to you—the weight of everything that is unresolved in your heart weighs you down. Because of my reading with Jennifer, I was able to set some of that burden aside.

Jennifer brought through my grandmother next—my dad's mom. Those were probably the two most important people and the most significant losses of my life. My dad had died first, and my grandmother passed years later. Everything Jennifer said about my grandmother was spot on, but you're always waiting for that "wow" thing, that one piece of evidence that lets you know that your loved one is undoubtedly there in the room with you.

Jennifer nailed it. "Tracey, your grandmother is showing me these biscuits. You know when a grandmother has biscuits, right? Remember the biscuits, remember the biscuits."

I knew the biscuits she meant immediately and began to cry a little. Even to this day, I make them every year for Christmas; they are called "angel biscuits." Throughout my childhood, my grandmother took a biscuit recipe and created these wonderful cinnamon rolls. That was my "wow" moment, when I felt for the first time with certainty that the afterlife is real. Jennifer told me things about my grandmother, like the fact that she had a college education. In those days, it was rare for a woman to be college educated. She also had a job—most women during that time were stay-at-home mothers, raising families. She told me how my grandmother had her hair done every Tuesday. She wore lipstick, and she would blot it on a tissue. We would always have tissues in the car with blotted lipstick. So much of the reading was very specific. Our strong connection together came through too. She was one of the two most important people in my life that had passed away. My grandmother was a small part of the reading, but an impactful part.

My grandfather came through as well. Jennifer gave a lot of specifics about him—that he was a hunter, had died of cancer, and raised doves. There's no denying it! Jennifer could never have known any of that.

One part of a medium's job is to give you things that wouldn't show up in a Google search. That's what we do. We give you a specific memory, and what their personalities were like. We give you specific pieces of evidence to prove that we have your loved ones with us. We give you the things that are not in an obituary. Our job is to prove that the afterlife is real and to provide healing.

At the end of the reading, after my dad, my grandmother, and my grandfather had come through, I had an aunt come through also. Her message was directly for my mom, and it was really interesting. Jennifer said, "Your aunt keeps talking about the boys. The boys, the boys." At that time, my mom and stepdad had taken in my stepdad's grandkids, because his daughter was suffering from drug addiction. So, my mom and stepdad, who were in their sixties, were raising two young boys. My mom and my aunt were very close; she came through showing support for my mom and to give her the message that they are there and watching over everyone.

I walked away from that reading so at peace and so comforted that I would never need another one again. That's just how life-changing a reading can be; I got the closure and connection that I needed. Some people will seek out mediums just once, some once a year, or several times a year. There is no wrong or right answer as to how often you should see a medium. Sometimes that first experience with a medium can be so impactful and healing that you don't need one again, because you get closure and proof of the afterlife. You receive all the things you need to move forward.

The power of mediumship, the impact of hearing from those on the other side, the possibility of healing through Spiritual connection was all brought home to me that day. I gained so much, and I will treasure that experience forever. I experienced the powerful healing of a medium, which I would never, ever, forget.

My Daughter's Reading

It wasn't until December of 2015 that I would seek out another medium. The reasons were different. In 2009, my daughter's best friend, Kara, who was sixteen, was killed by a drunk driver in a head-on collision. I can't begin to explain how devastating that was, especially to my daughter. Kara was a few years older, and she was getting ready to graduate and have her senior prom.

Kara was a firecracker. The whole energy of a room would sparkle the moment she walked in. She was a brown-haired, green-eyed "force to be reckoned with." She would walk in our house and say to me, "I'm here, Mom. Want to see my new T-shirt design?" She would always have some music with her and never lost a groove.

She and my daughter Jazmine had a strong connection to music. They loved Disco Curtis, Jonas Brothers, All Time Low, and Mayday Parade. Kara was vibrant, and full of life and love. That night in May, Kara decided to go to a concert of one of her favorite bands. Jazmine was supposed to go with her but changed her mind. For some reason, she decided to go to another event instead. Maybe it was insight or intervention protecting her. Maybe it just wasn't her time. That choice may have saved her life, but it also brought her a lot of guilt, heartache, and pain. Things happen for a reason, but Kara's death was so difficult to take, so hard to understand, that it took years before Jazmine found peace.

Kara and a friend were driving at about midnight on the Dallas North Tollway, heading home. She came around a curve on the one-way highway and was met by a large red truck going the wrong way. The truck was driven by a young mother who was studying to be a nurse. She had gone to a wedding that night and was unfamiliar with that side of town. She had gotten to the end of the tollway and didn't know where she was going. When she turned around, she entered the tollway going the wrong direction. They collided head-on, and Kara's journey on Earth came to an end that night, May 10, 2009.

We lived in Little Elm—a place where everyone knows everyone else. It is a tiny suburb with a small high school. Kara's death was felt by the whole town. It was a significant loss for the community, but even more significant for my daughter. It took her on a path of numbing, depression, and suicidal thoughts.

I became afraid to leave Jazmine at home. We decided to keep the garage door locked, so she couldn't pull a car into it and commit suicide. My daughter struggled a lot, and being a single mom at that time, I just didn't know how to help my child go through something like that. There are no training manuals that teach you how to help your child through such a trauma. I know, looking back now, that she feels as though she went through that alone. Grief is hard, but especially hard to watch as your child suffers through it. It was an extremely painful time. Several years later, Jazmine ended up moving to Lubbock. She followed her boyfriend, who went to college there. I knew she was still hurting and dealing with her pain.

One time when she came home, I thought to myself, "I've got to get her to a medium. I have to. Maybe that will heal her." I didn't know what else to do, I didn't feel that I could help her, but maybe Spirit could. I remember dragging her to another gallery event that Jennifer Farmer was putting on. Jazmine didn't know what to expect, and she wasn't thrilled about it. She went but sat with her arms crossed and just watched. Unfortunately, we did not get a message from Kara that day. It wasn't the right timing, perhaps, or maybe Jazmine wasn't ready yet.

Then in December of 2015, I was given the nudge again to seek out a medium for Jazmine. I mentioned earlier that every person I encountered had an impact on my journey, and that included my facialist named Stacy. When I first sat in her chair, she told me the story of her son, Dylan. He was fifteen or sixteen when he died of an overdose. He was Stacy's only child. We developed a stronger connection over time because my daughter Jazmine was suffering from the loss of her friend. Stacy told me that she saw a psychic once a year and it always helped her. She was much less expensive than Jennifer, and less well known, and it seemed like it was worth a try. Stacy had had some great experiences with her, and I was desperate to bring my daughter some closure.

I convinced Jazmine to go with me for a reading. She was a little bit more open to going this time. She was having problems with her boyfriend, and she agreed just to get some direction about him, and we prayed that Kara would come through as well. Her boyfriend, Zach, had his own trauma—his brother had been murdered, and I think that death and Kara's death brought these two souls together. (Twelve years later, they are still happy, and engaged to be married.)

We drove all the way out to Garland, Texas, and pulled up to an old 1970s home. We get out and go up to the house and knock, and Molly opens the door. We were welcomed by a warm, Latina woman with a grandmotherly demeanor—very different from Jennifer Farmer! And clearly from her deep, brown eyes, one could see she had a heart of gold. She took us to a room where she did her readings. It was just a spare bedroom with a couple of chairs and a table.

We sat down for the reading. Molly gave Jazmine a remarkable reading, including her relationship with Zach, his parents, and what problems she could expect in the future. She gave us a lot of great stuff, and then we finally asked, "Well, is there anybody here?"

"Yes," she said. "There's a girl, a young woman here with us."

I later learned that every psychic isn't a medium, but every medium is a psychic. There is a big difference that I didn't realize at the time. A medium is a person who can communicate with people who have passed away—either friends, family, or acquaintances of the sitter. The medium is truly the middle person between the sitter and the Spirit world. A psychic, on the other hand, works with the sitter's energy field to shed light on higher purpose, the future, past, and present. Both psychics and mediums offer hope, healing, and empowerment to the sitter.

Maybe all Jazmine needed to hear was that she was there. But something happened there that changed both of our lives' trajectories. At the end of the reading, Molly looked at Jazmine and said, "You know, you're gifted, and you can do this too." Upon hearing that, I froze—even now, I am overwhelmed just thinking about it. I had never thought of mediumship as something that ordinary people could actually do. Even after I had learned that there were psychics beyond the John Edwards and Sylvia Brownes of the world—people who were famous—I still hadn't thought of mediumship as something truly available to learn or pursue if you weren't some sort of chosen one. I had been watching all these medium shows. I had a passionate interest in mediumship, and even a calling in subtle ways, for years. But I didn't think I could do it because one had to be *special*. And then, here was a psychic telling us my daughter also has the gift.

It was a revelation to me. Jazmine can do this? Can anyone? Can I? Jazmine was told that she could do it, and that started her healing journey. It would take time, and would be difficult for her, but over the next couple of years, she started finding her way, healing, and moving forward with her own life. She's a medium now as well; Molly was right about that. That one encounter meant so much.

There are no coincidences. I was meant to meet Stacy, who introduced me to Molly, who told Jazmine about her psychic talent. We were meant to hear that message because it changed everything.

Jazmine's own journey would come a little bit later. At that time, she wasn't ready. What happens when you have a calling to do this work is that you no longer want to partake in things that hurt your body and soul. Jazmine just wasn't ready to give all that up yet. She was in too much pain. That was her journey. On the other hand, I *was* ready. This was only a month after my own healing journey had started, after I had awakened that morning, having been given a new energy and freed of my own self-destructive path. My journey had already started a month earlier—I just had not realized yet that the path I was on was leading me to become a psychic medium.

Opening Doors at Metaphysical Stores

I left that reading feeling pumped, changed, excited—every feeling I could possibly have. I wanted to learn everything I could about mediumship, and how I could further my journey. I couldn't wait to get home and find a metaphysical store to discover resources. I had no idea that such stores even existed before then, but I found one, just thirty minutes away from my house, and decided to go visit. Miracles of Joy was in a little building on a side road in Lewisville, Texas. As I entered the store and closed the door behind me, the wind chimes jingled magically. There I found everything that was missing for me in church. There were crystals and tarot cards, incense and candles, herbs, and sprays of flowers everywhere. From the minute I walked in, it felt that I was meant to be there. This was my new home, and it was exactly where I needed to be. That was how I was introduced to this new, wonderful oasis.

Miracles of Joy offered spiritual development classes. I was immediately interested and took every class I could. I encourage you to do the same if you have such a store nearby and have not done so yet. Explore Reiki, past lives, psychic or mediumship development, trances, or channeling.

The most impactful classes for me were the ones about psychic and mediumship development. My first teacher there was Jayme O'Donnell; I took every Saturday class that she offered. I was there for four hours every Saturday—two hours for psychic development, two hours for mediumship. It was the scariest thing of my life because I was continually tested on my abilities with the exercises. I would sit there in class so scared that I could hardly breathe, and thought, "Oh, my God, if I get it wrong, they're going to judge me negatively. Maybe I'm not gifted."

It is natural, of course, to second guess ourselves every single time, every step of the way on this journey. I would beat myself up every day after leaving, thinking, "Ugh, I am never going to get this . . . ." I have cried a lot of tears and have second-guessed my decision every day. But the one thing I didn't do was give up! Everyone has innate psychic abilities. I like to compare it to a marathon runner. Almost everybody can be a marathon runner, but not everyone is willing to do the work to be one. Anybody can be a medium, but you've got to be willing to do the work to be a medium.

There would be a lot of bad days on my journey, but when I had a really bad day, Spirit would give me these beautiful nuggets of magic as if to say, "Okay, she's had a rough time. I am going to give her a nugget." And they would give me something that was so right, so wow, it would make me say, "Yes! Yes!"

The learning process was intense, and I doubted myself constantly, but I felt as if I were being pulled by invisible forces stronger than myself. I was learning all the time—and often, we learn by failing, getting up, and trying again. I don't want you to think that this is something you'll never fail at, that you'll never get things wrong. You will. It will hurt, and you will doubt yourself and your journey. But you have to experience what it feels like to get it wrong, so that you understand what it feels like to get it right. And if you choose to stay on this path and develop your abilities, it can be one of the most rewarding things you'll ever do. The successes mean so much more than the failures that precede them.

Validation and a Conversation with God

By this time, I knew and trusted that I'd be a medium. That was the road that I was going to take, even though I was dipping my toes into everything. I needed to feel as though I was validated—that mediumship was meant to be my path. At the time, I was so new to this journey, and I so desperately wanted someone to validate for me that I was on the right path. I hear this a lot from my students and followers, "I have these gifts, but is this the right path for me?" We're all just looking for someone to validate us. If Molly hadn't validated that for Jazmine, I would have never even understood that I could do this work.

So, for my readers, let me validate your choice today: if you are reading this book, this is all the validation you need that this is a path. It is a chosen path, and once you embark on it, it becomes your path. God, Universe, Source, whatever you want to call it, will open doors for you, but it's up to you to walk through them. It is still free will. It is about the choices that you make.

We all have an ability to do something, but we're not all meant to do this work. It's not a calling for everyone, but if you are attracted to it, if you've been affected by death, or you are walking into metaphysical stores and feeling right at home, then it just might be. The choice is always yours, but know that it is not an easy road. It takes desire, dedication, discipline, and determination.

Early on in my development, I had a conversation with my Higher Power. I asked, "Am I supposed to do this? Is this my path? What would people think about me?" I would ask these questions because, at that time, I was still desperately looking for my purpose and hoping to have answers given to me, but I found that the answers all lie within. You have to figure out for yourself what your purpose is, and what's going to make you happy. For me, I knew there was a calling for me. I knew I had felt the healing power of mediumship. I knew that I would love to give that gift to other people, but I had to ask God, "Am I supposed to do this, and what will people think?"

As I sat there with God, I heard a response, "It doesn't matter what people think. What matters are the people you'll heal. That's all that matters. There will be tough days, but that's why we chose you."

I replied, "Well, why? Why me?"

God said, "I sent you many lessons, and even tragedy, and you were still resilient in your path, and you feel called. You were chosen because you can handle the times that will get tough, and for that, I grant you the stars."

I feel that we're called or have a calling because we were once broken, and we survived it. We survived and we're still here, still fighting towards our better selves, pulling towards a greater life. I could have gone down the road of drug addiction and lost everything, but I didn't. Drugs, yes, were part of my life. Difficult things happened to me, but I always managed to stay strong. I didn't allow anything to destroy me. It was a numbing mechanism for me, but I didn't end up on the streets and I didn't end up losing everything. Someone else may have experienced even greater hardship, and their strength might have been in returning from that place. Through all I experienced, I stayed resilient. I had a strength inside me that kept me going.

I want you to know there will be hard times. You will be challenged. You will cry. You will wonder why you have even chosen this. I always say that mediumship is the hardest and most rewarding experience I've ever had. That's what keeps me going—it is the experiences I have that fuel me. If you're meant to do it, you'll know. You won't want to give up. You'll go through the hard times, put yourself out there to be ridiculed, judged, and called *crazy*. You'll put yourself out there and be wrong sometimes, and that's okay. If you're resilient and you don't give up, this is definitely a worthy path, and it is attainable. You can do this.

Divine Timing and Findlay College

Divine timing is one of the validations you are on the right track.

At that time of my awakening, I was a single mother with young adults still living at home who were starting their own families. It was a tough time financially, and I was doing it all alone. Running a household on one income was a struggle, so I didn't have extra money to spend on pursuing my psychic studies.

That is where divine timing came in. When my grandmother passed away in 2016, she left our family some oil rights in West Texas. We were soon approached by someone asking to buy the rights, which had been in our family for a long time. My siblings and I decided that we didn't know if this opportunity would come again, so we went ahead and sold them. It was significant money for me, especially at the time. The timing was, indeed, divine.

I now had the means for my new-found "hobby." It was also during this time that the husband of one of my best friends got a job as a vice-president for a very large bank in London, England. They had just moved there when I came into this money, so I decided to visit them for a month. It was not a cheap excursion; the airline tickets alone to London were over $2,000, so this would never have been possible before. Prior to this, I was scraping together gas money at the end of every month. Now I had the means and the opportunity, since my children were all grown.

My friends at Miracles of Joy all knew that I was going to England, so they asked me if I had ever heard of Arthur Findlay College. I had not, but they told me that Arthur Findlay is a college just outside of London that trains mediums.

Well, unbeknownst to me, Spiritualism is a recognized religion in England. Using Spiritualism, they train and develop mediums to be a part of their churches. Every Sunday service includes a medium getting up and proving life after death. One of the pioneers of Spiritualism, Arthur Findlay, left his beautiful old mansion to the church, and it became a training center for evidential proof of life after death.

The college offers several different kinds of short-term courses, typically, seven days at a time. They have dorm rooms for the students and provide breakfast, lunch, and dinner every day in between classes. As soon as I heard about this place, I knew I had to go. I checked their website and chose a course that was headed by Paul Jacobs. I had no idea who he was, or what I was getting myself into. I took a huge leap of faith and booked my stay. What I didn't realize was that students book these courses a year in advance, so I was really lucky to get in and have a room to stay in.

I was going to London—and to Arthur Findlay College—just to see if I was a medium! I booked a course without having any real prior training, and no knowledge of any of the tutors. I took that leap on blind faith because something inside of me told me that I had to go. I was learning, from this and prior experiences, to just listen to where I am being led. I learned not to overthink it—and to never let fear stop me. When we start listening, we realize, indeed, we are being led divinely.

My journey has led me to trust my intuition, trust my guides, and trust where providence leads me. I've learned to not second-guess things. Sometimes people will get an idea, and they will overanalyze it. I lean into it. That's what I have learned, and I don't know where it came from. Even buying my house. The first one I saw, I bought, because it just felt right. That's become a recurring theme for me, especially since my journey started. I don't question things that I know, even when I don't know how I know them. I just feel that if I've got to go, I am going. God gave me the money to go to England to visit my friend. So I never questioned it. Everything

I needed just lined up, one thing after another—the money, my friend's invitation, the college—each exactly what I needed to put me where I needed to be next.

I think that Spirit puts ideas in our heads, and we can interrupt the flow of inspiration if we overthink it. If people would just let the ideas come, and go for it, there would be much more success in this world. But if you're going to let your left brain come in and overthink it, it will tell you every reason why you shouldn't do it, why you're not good enough, and why it's a bad idea. If you're going to let fear stand in your way, you won't progress. I believe Spirit is talking to us all the time. I believe our guides are continually trying to give us little snips of direction, but sometimes we get in the way of their messages.

As much as possible, I try to be open to possibilities that come into my life, and trust fate and intuition. I approach everyone I meet, and every situation I find myself in, as part of this divine plan, as something or someone that may have been sent to me to help me on my journey. I look for the meaning and purpose behind them, trusting Spirit, and letting the Universe guide me. I have my eyes wide open for possibilities unfolding all around me. And when something feels right, I say "yes" as quickly and as passionately as I can.

Manifestation

So much of what happened to me during this time was synchronicity, meeting the right person at the right time, or being pushed to be in the right place at the right time. It all served a purpose—leading me to where I needed to be. The Universe was nudging me along.

But you can make that work in reverse, as well. You can let the Universe know where you want to go and nudge it in the direction of your choosing. That's where manifestation comes in. You set the goal and let the Universe help bring it to you. You want to follow where you're being led in life, and you want to let life know where you want to be going. They work together.

Let's do an exercise in manifestation. Use your journal and write down what you want your life to look like, or what you want to happen in the next year. This can be something to do with a relationship, your career, or where you want to live. The possibilities are endless, and I'll leave this up to you as to where you want to focus your attention.

Manifestation can be a strong tool, and it can be very powerful. Since you're reading this book, you're starting to raise your vibration, and develop your spiritual gifts. As your vibration rises, you will start to become happier because you're shedding all those things that no longer serve you—including all the trauma and abuse. All your old stories and negative patterns start to fall away at this point in your journey. Your vibration is rising, and you are feeling lighter and happier. You are going to start attracting the kinds of things that are similar to you in your life. Using the manifestation tool can be very powerful because now you're starting to make the most of your potential.

Let's look at an example in the form of romance. If you're looking to bring someone romantically into your life, list everything that you want out of a relationship. Get as detailed as you possibly can, and state it as if it is fact: *I am in this relationship with this person.* Detail the physical traits, the personality, and the qualities that are most special to you. What are the person's interests and hobbies? Get very specific and write it all down so that the Universe knows there is no question that this is exactly who you are looking for. State it as a fact, and then watch how the Universe responds. You will likely be surprised by what comes into your life, as long as you take action to help make it happen. Manifestation is two-fold. You must take steps to realize your deepest wishes, and then allow the Universe to respond to you.

This can also go for money, or almost anything. Create positive beliefs about yourself and the Universe. Live and act from a place of confidence and happiness and notice the opportunities that the Universe is providing you. Have the faith to act on them when they are presented to you. Embrace the best of life and live as the best version of yourself. You can state clearly to yourself, in your journal, exactly how you want it to be. Then take action to get it, putting yourself in the place to accomplish or find it. You will discover that the Universe will start bringing those things to you more and more. You'll start meeting the right people, finding job opportunities, and making connections everywhere. You can create almost anything you want in your life.

Here are a few examples of what *manifesting* statements might look like:

Money
I have abundance in my life.
Checks are showing up in the mail.
I am financially prosperous.
My business is booming.
I work where I want with people I want.

Love

I am attracting healthy love.

I am loved more than I ever thought possible.

The Universe is sending me my soul mate.

I attract love.

You might notice that many of these statements sound like positive affirmations—those positive phrases and statements mentioned in "Chapter Two: Loving Affirmations and Gratitude" that are repeated to challenge negative thoughts and encourage positive changes in your life.

The core difference is that the intention of manifesting statements is to not only change your mindset, but to actually bring something tangible into your life through attraction and belief. *If you think it, it will come.*

Let's take this statement: *I am attracting the perfect person for me.*

As an affirmation, the intention of this phrase is to change your limiting belief that you always attract the wrong man/woman. The manifesting intention of the same phrase is to find the right partner. That is, you are single, and you want to date again after a divorce. You have worked on yourself, and you are wanting someone that would be perfect for you. Affirmations change the way you think, and manifesting statements draw things into your life via the Law of Attraction.

Here is an example if you want to manifest a specific love interest in your life. Write down exactly what you want. For example, here is my list:

Desirable Traits

Compassionate

Kind

Loyal

Attentive

Dependable

Non-controlling

Has stable job

Has been through some things and understands healing

Loves to dance

Will dance with me in the kitchen

Loves to travel

Loves family

Craft a few manifesting statements of your own.

Starting in this very moment, you can change your life forever for the better. And as you do, you gain more tools and insight to help the people you will be working with as you cultivate your skills as a psychic medium. The higher your vibration, the more service you are to others, and the clearer the channel for connecting to the afterlife.

CHAPTER FIVE

I AM A MEDIUM

The bonds of love are what connect us to the other side.
-John Edwards

Arthur Findlay College in the United Kingdom trains some of the world's best mediums. The college was established by members of the Spiritualist Church. Providing proof of life after death is a foundational principle of the Spiritualist religion. As it is a recognized religion in the United Kingdom, the development of mediumistic skills is also respected and accepted there—unlike the United States, where these abilities are not valued or even considered credible.

I was very drawn to Spiritualism because it was true to so many things that I believed—my values and viewpoints. It's probably the religion that fits me best, in many ways. Perhaps because it is not widely practiced in America, I've never felt pulled to join it. As part of my experience at Findlay College, however, it will forever hold a special place in my heart.

Spiritualists have seven principles that they believe in:

1. God is our Father.

2. We all belong to the brotherhood of man.

3. We can be blessed by a communion of Spirits and a ministry of angels.

4. The human soul exists continuously.

5. We each have and must accept personal responsibility.

6. We receive compensation and retribution in the hereafter for all the good and evil deeds done on Earth.

7. All of us can enjoy eternal progress of our human soul.

These are the principles and foundations of Spiritualism that the college teaches. Arthur Findlay College is open to everyone who wants to develop, but it is guided by Spiritualist beliefs. Students are taught how to connect with Spirit and how to give evidence of life after death in front of a congregation. It's very different from most of the mediumship taught in the United States.

My time as an Arthur Findlay student helped me along my path toward mediumship and increased the confidence that I had in my abilities. I learned the importance of building divine power by "sitting in the power." I also learned the importance of building a relationship with the Spirit world and how we are of service to those who dwell in the Spirit world. I discovered the importance of evidence, connecting to the sitter, and bringing one's whole self to the work. At Findlay, I established a deep trust in Spirits so that I could share exactly what I received from them, rather than trying to change the message into what *I* think would make more sense.

I fostered greater insight into mediumship and myself during that time.

Here are some of the jewels from Findlay that I would like to share with you so that you, too, can discover your capabilities as a medium.

Arrival

I knew almost nothing about Arthur Findlay College in April of 2016, when I boarded my American Airlines flight to London. I was scared of everything; I had never traveled alone outside the country. It was frightening, to say the least, but I did it. I just listened to my intuition and took a leap of faith—and did it without overthinking. I was committed to learning how to be a medium. I had been given the opportunity, and I was going to see it through, fearful or not.

I landed at Heathrow Airport and then had to take a two-hour bus ride to Stansted Airport. At the desk, I met a girl named Agnes, from Hungary. She was also going to Findlay, and we decided to share a taxi ride to the school.

"This is my third time coming for classes," Agnes said, as we rode the taxi through the streets and alleyways of the little town of Stansted.

"This is my first time." I watched as we pulled into the long driveway of the huge, old, stone and brick building. The facade had numerous columns and arches that made the mansion seem palatial. The grounds, too, were majestic. Beautiful lawns as far as the eye could see opened to groves of ancient oak trees, surrounded by flowers, and horses grazing. The beauty before me was just how I had imagined the English countryside would be with its stone and wooden buildings with latticed windows, picturesque fields, and abundant gardens.

Agnes and I walked up the stairs and entered the main building. I was ushered into a small receptionist area, and we were given our room assignments. With room keys in hand, we headed upstairs in a tiny elevator. The elevator stopped once before it reached our floor, and in stepped a tall, blonde man, with suits hanging over his shoulder—very distinguished-looking. The three of us were crammed together very closely in the elevator, so I decided to reach out to him. Assuming he was also a student, I said to him, "Have you been here before?"

"Yes, many times," he said humbly with an English accent.

I thought to myself, "Aw . . . he is so sweet and nice." He got off the elevator, and Agnes chuckled to herself in the corner.

"What? Why are you laughing?" I asked.

"Don't you know who he is?" she asked incredulously.

"I have no idea who he is. Isn't he a student?" My face clearly showed my confusion.

"No, that's Tony Stockwell," she giggled again. "He's a famous medium here in England. He even has a television show."

That tells you how green I was as a medium; Tony Stockwell is, indeed, one of the best-known mediums in the world, and I didn't even know who he was! I turned beet red from embarrassment, and that's how my trip started.

We arrived at our floor and went to our own separate rooms. The rooms resembled little dorms; my room had three twin beds in it and a sink. One by one, my new roommates arrived. The first one, Emma, was like an English version of Lucille Ball—very animated, with long burgundy hair and blunt bangs. Emma was a nurse who lived in England and drove one of those small, charming English cars.

We unpacked and put everything away. Next, we had to wait in a long line to interview with the tutors, who would determine which one of them would be the best match for our experience and personalities. We were each then called separately into a room with all the tutors. I was terrified when it got to my turn. All those feelings of unworthiness flooded my brain. What if I am not worthy of being here? Who am I to say I want to be a medium? "Just face it, Tracey," I thought to myself, "You have only been taking classes since January and we're in April. You've had virtually no training at all!"

Over a hundred mediums had arrived at the college to attend sessions while I was there. I was immersed with mediums from all over the world. It was really magical, as I glanced around the room at people from China, Australia, Hungary, England, and other places. It was just crazy to me! I'd never met with a medium in my life except for Jennifer Farmer, and now suddenly, I was in another country, surrounded by them. I was so nervous!

Once it was my turn, I found myself at a table with five tutors on the other side. I had no idea who they were. A slender, bald man, who was very matter of fact, introduced himself as Paul Jacobs. There was another tall, slender man with a very unique mustache that was long and curled at the end, and who dressed rather sharply. His name was Andy Byng. Then, there was Jackie Wright, a very distinguished English woman who had light reddish-blonde hair down to her shoulders. Last, there was John Johnson, a handsome man, lean, and bald.

I would say that the tutors at Findlay are the best of the best in the world. They are very disciplined in their service to the Spirit world. The connections they have are strong, and the evidence they provide is outstanding. They are consistently working on their mediumship and dedicate themselves to training others.

"Have you had any training?" Paul Jacobs asked me.

I replied, "No, no training. I am just here. Just beginning. I just want to learn all I can, but don't know anything, really. I want to learn it all!" That hunger to learn, that desire to take in as much as I possibly could, was so strong, I wanted to experience everything they had to offer. They decided to put me with Jackie Wright, in the beginner/intermediate class, and that turned out to be a perfect first experience for me at Findlay.

Jackie was teaching a more intermediate-level course that week, but something told the faculty that she was the tutor for me. I would go on to spend the next seven days with seventeen other people who were in her class. That's how it works at Arthur Findlay—you stay with the same tutor for the entire week. Every day, students meet with their class at different places in the college, in different libraries and rooms, with every room being unique. One massive library had dark shelves all the way around the room, full of old books. There was, for example, the "green room," which had different shades of the color green throughout it, from the carpet to the walls, complemented with floral patterns everywhere. Each room was different and beautiful, and they all had a rich history of their own, which added to the mystique. I found myself completely fascinated by this, and I immersed myself in discovering more about the school.

Because the experience was so grand, and the energy there was so immense and strong, I didn't miss the television, my regular life, or anything else. When I was not in training, I wandered around outside, soaking in the lush, peaceful countryside. Every day, I was surrounded by people working on their spiritual journeys through their study of mediumship. Everyone was there to learn and to practice connecting to Spirit. It was very powerful to be surrounded by people who believed, who knew, and who walked this path daily.

In Texas, mediumship was a fringe topic, something that most people didn't really know about, much less believe in. Even as someone who was pursuing it, it was still a small part of my life. Every day, life provided an endless number of distractions. I still had to show up as a mom, wife, and employee. However, while at the college, I could escape all of that and dive deep into my longing. My passion for mediumship was shared by the people in my dorm. There were endless conversations with other students during breakfast and lunch, in every room and every class—virtually every hour spent there! Connecting to the afterlife for six hours a day can be draining, challenging, and emotional, but so profoundly rewarding.

Jackie Wright and Confirmation

I was privileged to spend seven days as a student with Jackie Wright. We learned the importance of "sitting in the power" and building energetic power. Throughout the day, Jackie would pair us up, and give us short exercises to help us connect psychically with each other. It wasn't too threatening and was a fun way of getting to know my fellow students.

On day two, Jackie walked into the classroom and said, "Who here has never connected with Spirit?" I looked around the room, and not one hand was raised. I was very anxious and wondered to myself if I should. After about a second of internal dialogue with myself, I decided to be brave, and raised my hand. At that point in time, I'd only been to classes since January. I didn't really know what I was doing, or if I was ever connecting. I managed to stammer out, "I've never done it . . . uh . . . I don't think . . . ."

"Great, come on up here," Jackie said. As I stood up, I thought that she was going to show me by doing it herself. Then she said, "I want you to stand next to me."

"Okay," I said, drawing closer to her.

The next thing she said was, "Shut your eyes."

"Huh?" At this point, my heart was starting to pound and felt as if it was ready to pop out of my chest.

Again, she directed me, "Shut your eyes."

I surrendered and said, "Okay . . . ." and took a deep breath in.

"I want you to picture a door and tell me who's standing there."

I was in front of seventeen people and the tutor, having never done this before, terrified. My ability and I were being put on the spot—a combination of the fear one might feel while speaking publicly and simultaneously answering a pop quiz. I was so afraid that I was going to fail—that I was going to prove, right then and there, that I didn't know what I was doing—or worse, that I could never do it.

I took a deep breath and listened closely to Jackie.

She said, "Is it a man or is it a woman?"

"It is a woman."

"Who is this woman to someone here in the classroom?"

I got a feeling and said, "It is somebody's mom."

"Now I want you to feel this mother," she drew in closer to me, almost whispering. "Tell me what she liked to do."

"She loved to cook for her family," I said, thinking I was just making things up.

"But what is it? Big dinners? Or are they little dinners?"

"No, when she cooks, she cooks big. That's her way of showing love. She likes to cook big."

"What else did this lady do?" Jackie persisted.

"She likes to make cards." I didn't even know where those words came from; they just popped into my head, all of a sudden.

Jackie inquired, "How did this lady die?" I got a tingle in my stomach and said, "Something with the stomach. She had stomach issues. There was something wrong with her stomach."

"Open your eyes, Tracey, and scan the room. Tell me who this lady belongs to."

I opened my eyes and glanced across the room, and then was drawn to a woman to my right center, and I said, "She belongs to her." And the lady just nodded her head "yes," as tears filled her eyes.

"Yes, that's my mom."

Jackie then turned to me and said, "Give her a name that would be important." I said, "Michael." And the lady that I identified began to shed more tears.

Michael was the name of her husband who had just passed away. I couldn't believe that I had actually done it! I stood in front of the whole class, scared out of my mind, thinking I was completely making things up, and I connected with Spirit. I connected with Gillian's mom. I was given evidence, and I brought it through to someone who needed it. As soon as that class was over, I ran up to my dorm room and started writing in my journal: "I am a medium. I am a medium. I am a medium."

I went to Findlay for proof that I could do it. That moment became my confirmation. I started using it as an affirmation: "I am a medium." I wrote it down everywhere and repeated it until I truly believed it: I *am* a medium.

I returned to Arthur Findlay three more times to fully live up to this new reality. I had found a community where I could grow with others who were as deeply committed as I was to this new, incredible path in my life.

John Johnson and the Soul of a Medium

The second time I took classes at Findlay, I enrolled in a class with a man who calls himself "The Natural Medium"—John Johnson. He defines "natural mediumship" as the ability through unfoldment, a gradual development or revelation, to be your true self. From him, I learned that effective mediumship is not just connecting to Spirit and spitting out information, it is putting one's heart and soul into it, and connecting deeply with the sitter. The medium's responsibility is to give the sitter what the soul needs to hear. It's not about fulfilling a checklist; it is very powerful and deeply introspective. John Johnson taught us to connect with the person's soul, feel what is needed in the moment, and bring that connection into our readings.

This is where there's a bit of crossover between a medium and a psychic. As I mentioned in Chapter Four, a medium is a person who can communicate with people who have passed away—either friends, family, or acquaintances of the sitter. The medium is truly the middle person between the sitter and the Spirit world. A psychic, on the other hand, works with the sitter's energy field. That is, a psychic connects with the energy field of the sitter to shed light on higher purpose, the future, past and present, and whatever appears as the soul's concerns and teachings for that day. Both psychics and mediums offer hope, healing, and empowerment to the sitter.

Those are my underlying reasons for doing this work. You'll hear along your journey that every medium is a psychic, but not every psychic is a medium, and that's exactly how it works. To be a medium, you have to have both the facility to connect with the soul of the sitter and the Spirit that wishes to communicate with that person. In psychic readings, it is soul-to-soul direct communication with the sitter; in mediumship, it is connection from "above" with the world beyond the veil.

There are many different types of mediumship. There is evidential mediumship, which is what I do and what they teach at Findlay

College. Evidential mediumship is about *proving* the afterlife. We come up with evidence for the sitter of the deceased person's life, personality, and specific memories to prove that their loved one is sitting with us during the session.

There is also trance mediumship, where mediums actually surrender completely and allow Spirit to come into the body, or at least really close to the body. This means that any words coming out of the medium's mouth come completely from Spirit. During trance mediumship, people's facial expressions, mannerisms, speech patterns, and voice can change. Each medium offers a different approach; all have many of the same elements but come through in slightly different ways. Each medium has his or her own way to best connect to Spirit and the sitter.

John Johnson was teaching evidential mediumship, but his focus was on the soul connection, on the meaning side of the work. Yes, you're delivering messages to the sitter, or memories from Spirit, but you're doing it for the sitter's own journey and healing. As a medium, you're connecting to Spirit, but you're offering more than just information. You are opening up on a heart level, to bring your full self to the sitter and to the work. It's not just something you do, but in a more profound sense, it is an act of service—giving your all to it and bringing heart, mind, and Spirit fully to the sitter. John Johnson taught me about touching upon the feelings of people, letting them know that, yes, mediums are there to communicate with the afterlife, but we are also there to offer healing.

I also learned from him that "whatever is wrong in your mediumship is what is wrong within you." It was a huge lesson. For example, I had struggled with my confidence in my mediumship. When I heard John Johnson say those words, I knew then that I had something to heal within me. I would never be confident in my mediumship until I became confident within myself.

Andy Byng and Trusting the Message

On my third trip to Findlay College, Andy Byng was my tutor. Andy Byng is known as the "mustache man" because of his large, black, handlebar mustache. He has an exceptional way of teaching and connecting to students. One of the most powerful experiences that I had under Andy's tutelage was when he sat us all in a circle and said, "I want you to connect to somebody in Spirit. When you get your first visual, I want you to state who you've got and what the visual means."

I sat there and then felt a strong presence as I connected. I felt as though I was communicating with a grandfather, and he shows me a monkey. It looked like a pet monkey. It had a leash and that seemed crazy to me. When it got to my turn to say what I saw, I said, "I have a grandfather." And because my brain said, "There's no way that anybody could have a pet monkey," I changed it and I said, "I have a grandfather who collected monkey figurines." That seemed like something that was more likely, and maybe it made more sense. No one in the circle identified with my connection. As I looked around the room, blank stares were looking back at me.

Then Andy turned to me again, "Tracey, what did you *see*?"

"Well, I saw a grandfather who showed me a monkey."

He smiled lightly and asked, "What kind of monkey?"

"It looked like a pet monkey. It had a leash and everything."

"Why didn't you say pet monkey?" he cocked his head, deeply interested.

"Because who has a pet monkey?"

And then he stared right into my eyes, "My grandfather had a pet monkey."

I couldn't believe what I was hearing! Had I just made a connection with the tutor's own grandfather?

I learned that day to never change what Spirit gives me. I learned that a psychic must never over-interpret the messages—just give the sitter what you get. Spirit is never wrong; we, as mediums, can get it wrong because our brain takes the message and makes it into something else, all because we don't trust. This taught me about the importance of complete surrender to what Spirit gives me. It also taught me not to be afraid to say it.

I think that everyone who is studying to become a medium starts out being afraid of getting it wrong so that few actually recognize what they're seeing. I was still afraid of getting "nos" when I was taking Andy's class, so it was a great lesson for me to learn. Sometimes you just have to take the ego out of it, report what you get, and not worry about the outcome.

If you water things down to make them "safe" or more palatable, you can lose those powerful "yeses." When we start working together in this book to develop your psychic and medium skills, always trust what you see and what you're being told, and be as complete and honest as you can. You are a messenger. It's not your job to write the message. Your duty is to deliver it. You have to learn that "nos" are part of the process. Allow yourself to be a little bit fearless when it comes to communicating what you see. Be willing to be vulnerable and honest, follow where Spirit leads you, and trust the message. You never know when a pet monkey might actually be . . . a pet monkey!

Andy Byng and Following Where Spirit Leads

Andy Byng led us in an exercise in which we each stood in front of the class, one at a time. My instructions were to connect with a Spirit and identify the person in the room to whom it "belonged." I'll make note here that this is an integral part of the training at Arthur Findlay. They train mediums to stand in front of congregations at Spiritualist churches, connect with Spirit and bring them through. Part of that training is to know how to identify the member of the congregation that the Spirit belongs to, also known as "going direct." In the United States, we call this a *gallery-type* reading or *platform* reading. It is considered advanced mediumship in America, but it is taught as a fundamental skill at Arthur Findlay.

At this part of my journey, I wasn't fully confident just yet. Typically, Andy would stand next to the newer students to help guide them. As I stood up in front of the class, he stood by my side, guiding me while I made my connection. "Tracey, who do you have?" he asked.

"I have a father who is here for his daughter in the audience," I replied.

"Good. Tell me what this dad showed you." He came closer to me while he looked out at the faces of my classmates.

"He showed me a Rubik's Cube." Andy nodded his head and said, "Okay, let's talk about this for a second. Does anybody have a dad in Spirit who would understand the Rubik's Cube?"

Three people raised their hands. At this point, I was dying with nervousness. My armpits were sweating. My knees were shaking. The others could hear the trembling in my voice. Even though I had done this before, and despite everything I had learned, confidence was still lacking for me. That's why trust and vulnerability are such big parts of the mediumship journey. You can't do this and not be putting yourself out there. You have to learn to stand in that moment, with all that uncertainty and doubt, and let Spirit take you where you are meant to go.

Andy continued, "Tracey, where is this Rubik's Cube?"

Closing my eyes, I saw an image of the cube in a professional setting. "In an office . . . ."

"Let's go further. Where in this office?"

"On a shelf . . . ."

"Good. Okay. What's it next to?"

"It's next to a picture frame."

Andy said, "Okay. Who's in the picture?"

"The dad and somebody else."

At that moment, I got stuck. I looked closely at the image of the Rubik's Cube, then the office. I visualized the picture frame and the Rubik's Cube on the shelf. I needed some help. Andy then stepped in next to me and created a "double link."

A double link is when two people link into the same Spirit. Andy has years of experience and sees more clearly than I can, so he could take the connection even further.

He asked the group of students, "Who can understand the Rubik's Cube next to the photo of your father with Bill Gates?" The Chinese girl in the audience raised her hand. Her dad was a programmer for Apple and was right in the middle of that high-tech business world. Somehow, he had a photo of himself with Bill Gates proudly displayed on his bookshelf. Andy could see details that I had not perceived.

That's how I learned to go deep, to keep following an image or message and take it further, knowing that something powerful might be just a step or two away. I felt a dad who had a Rubik's Cube and died of a heart attack. That's where the baby medium in me stopped. Andy taught me to follow the evidence, ask questions, and allow Spirit to lead me deeper. If you just keep going, the entire reading can hinge on a single memory, just one piece of evidence that touches someone's heart. As you begin readings, do not wait for every drop of information to come in. Take the image that Spirit gives and unfold the story.

Everything I learned at Findlay helped me. I grew as a medium; I grew as a person. My confidence in my abilities, and in Spirit, grew tremendously. I found out that I could really do this work, that I wasn't making it up, and that it was real. I discovered I *am* a medium and made friends for life who shared in the wonder of this work.

I wish for you the same sense of belonging and certainty that I found there. There is nothing to be afraid of in the world of Spirit. Take every class you can locally, and eventually go on to find teachers in the United States—and even abroad—to continue your journey. Open yourself to learning. The world of mediumship awaits you.

CHAPTER SIX

SO YOU WANT TO BE A MEDIUM

You must find the place inside yourself where nothing is impossible.
-Deepak Chopra

I have now brought you along on my journey to mediumship. I hope that you've started on your own path of healing and learning to connect to Spirit. If, right now, you don't feel confident that you can do this work, or you don't feel validated or qualified, please trust me that you can do it! That's why you were drawn to this book, and why Spirit brought you here. You *can* do this.

For the rest of the book, I will share with you some practices and exercises that will strengthen your abilities and connect to Spirit. I'll also teach you how to start working with clients and give you some examples of what you might encounter during readings. You will discover how to show up in the world as a professional medium by believing in yourself and letting others believe in you.

In this chapter, I will introduce you to the idea of spirit guides, and teach you how to connect with them, so they can better help you on your journey. You can do all these exercises on your own.

Pay attention to finding which ones work best for you. If you feel compelled to modify them, feel free to do so. Remember, this is your journey, and Spirit is with you. You are not only practicing specific techniques, but you're also working on trusting and being open to where Spirit guides you.

Take time with each of these ideas, not only to practice them, but to sit with them and think on them. Don't expect results right away (although you may get them!), but work on bringing your intention to them. Be open to signs, feelings, and interpretations of what you receive. At first, even if it is only a feeling or a word, look for meaning in what you're given, and keep at it.

Connecting to Spirit requires faith, commitment, and showing up to do the work. The reward of opening a channel to higher planes and receiving messages from beyond is well worth overcoming the challenges on the path.

Let's begin.

Owning and Growing Your Power

One of the main disciplines I learned from my years at Arthur Findlay College was a tool called "sitting in the power." Sitting in the power is different from meditation. Sitting in the power takes the idea of quiet and focus and follows a completely different path. You start in much the same place as meditation; however, instead of focusing on the physical body and mind to achieve calmness and peace, your focus and awareness is on your own energetic power. Sitting in the power means sitting in your own divine power to increase your access to the spiritual realm. The purpose of sitting in the power is to understand your own power and energy—to build that power and sustain that power to improve your connection to the spirit realm.

If you think of yourself with an aura around you, that's your power. Sitting in the power is sitting in the divine place of your own power. We all know it takes energy to connect with the afterworld. Mediumship is about energy meeting energy. In order to sustain that energy, you have to work up the power to do that. You're not *trying* to connect with Spirit. You're not *trying* to meditate. You're not *trying* to do anything. When you sit in power, deeply experience your soul strength, your aura, your ability, and that unshakeable core at your center. Feel *your own power* and work to raise the vibrational power to a higher level.

When you do the exercise of sitting in the power, close your eyes, and visualize a glowing aura that completely envelops you. Visualize it as white light, or a golden energy, or whatever visual signifies strength to you. Then, expand your power by visualizing this aura growing larger and larger around you, as you expand its boundaries. See it growing steadily, in waves or pulses, expanding with every breath you take.

What you want to focus on is the feeling of your power growing and increasing. Continue pushing your power upwards and outwards, and extending it until it touches the wall and then the ceiling. Then you push your power out into the street and up through the roof, so you are creating a huge bubble of power. You are growing your power and learning to tap into it. Concentrate and increase it even further. In time, your mind will accept just how powerful you truly are. You will experience being far bigger and more powerful than your body.

Here are steps for sitting in your power:

1. Close your eyes. Concentrate on your breath as you inhale and exhale. Inhale and exhale and focus on your chest as it moves in and out. Inhale and exhale.

2. Become aware of your surroundings and physical body. Become aware of what is beneath you and in front of you. Move into a state of complete awareness.

3. Become aware of any tensions in the body. Breathe in and exhale, releasing any tensions in the body. Completely relax as you breathe in and out.

4. Next, visualize a pure white ball of light (the size of a quarter) floating in front of you. See a beautiful white light beaming from this round ball of energy. This light represents your power—your connection to the divine energy source.

5. As you continue to breathe in and out, imagine this white light expanding with every breath. Breathe in, breathe out.

6. Imagine this pure white energy filling your body from your head to your toes.

7. Imagine this white light energy filling every muscle, organ, and cell of your body.

8. Now visualize this white light extending outside the body and forming an aura around you. This is your energy field.

9. Imagine now that you have the ability to expand this white light by pushing it out to the walls of the room you are in. Now push it up to the ceiling. Fill the entire room with your power.

10. Now imagine expanding your power (light) past the walls of your room and filling the entire house you are in with that light.

11. Expand the light even further, down the block, around the corner, filling block by block, until the entire city is filled with your light. Expand now beyond the city, to neighboring cities, then to the entire state, country, and world.

12. Continue to expand your light to the Universe—blending, connecting, and harmonizing with pure Source energy—the Creator of all there is. Spend some time in this power of divine energy, and in your own power. Stay in this place for a few minutes.

13. When you are done, you can slowly start bringing in your light from the Universe, world, country, state, city, blocks, your home, your room, and finally containing your power within you. You have just experienced sitting in your own power.

For a guided meditation on sitting in the power, check out "The New Ultimate Sitting in the Power Exercise" by Helen Davita on YouTube.

Probably one of the most important factors in your development is discipline; you must have discipline to do this work. Schedule a time to do this exercise multiple times a week, consistently, to increase your strength and power, so that your connection to Spirit can become stronger. The goal of sitting in the power is to create a powerful-enough connection so that information flows easily to you. You're going to need that strength to do this work. You want to be able to bring that energy to your sessions so you can bring through more information and create more healing through your mediumship.

The stronger and more whole you become, the higher the level at which you will be able to work. It is an amazing experience. Like so much on the path to mediumship, it can be difficult. It will take dedication and determination on your part. However, you will discover how rewarding it is to feel your ability grow, and to know that you are capable of far more than you ever imagined.

Meditation will continue to be an important part of your journey as well. Meditation is so critical—it allows you to enter creative and intuitive mental states, quieting the more analytical left brain. Meditation also will deepen your trust in your perceptions even when your more-analytical mind fights them—in those moments when you might want to change the pet monkey into a monkey figurine. However, both meditation and sitting in the power give you the tools to bypass the chatter and doubt so you tap into different parts of your mind and your connection to Spirit. Make room in your life for both these practices. You will learn to calm your mind so you can sit comfortably with the unknown, and so you can feel and increase your power for the work you do. Think of meditation as an openness and a oneness with everything that comes to you or passes through you. Think of sitting in power as becoming a beacon that gets stronger and larger as it shines out to fill the world.

Raising Your Vibration

Raising your vibration is another part of your developmental journey, and it comes naturally, through your healing process. At this point, with the work you're doing with healing, affirmations, letting go of negativity, and allowing yourself love and happiness—all those actions are raising your vibration. The more you raise your vibration, the more joy and happiness you invite into your life.

Vibration is an oscillation of parts, or of an electromagnetic wave. We are all energy, and everybody and everything vibrates at a frequency. Even rocks have energy—and they vibrate too! That's why some people are attracted to crystals; it's all about energy and vibration. You may have noticed that sometimes you can feel other people's vibrations. If you've ever walked into a room and you sensed that someone was angry, that was their negative vibration you sensed. You want your own vibration to become positive and strong. You want to be radiating the happiness, strength, and love that you are bringing into your life, and sending it out to the Universe and everyone around you.

Again, like attracts like. If you are sitting in a low vibration where you're angry all the time, where you feel victimized and powerless, you're going to attract negative things to you. Your attention is focused on the things that you don't want. Whatever you put your attention on will grow. Whatever you're looking for, that's what you'll find.

That's why it is so important to raise your vibration. Look for the good in life, practice gratitude and affirmations, let go of hate, and allow yourself to love and be happy. This is especially important as you're looking to channel the afterworld. You don't want to bring all that negativity with you to your readings or to your Spirit connection.

As you heal and let go of fear, blame, and traumas, and you practice forgiveness and gratitude—all aspects of creating happiness—you naturally start raising your vibration. People will notice; people in my life say they've never seen me as happy as I am now. Never. And it is because I've done the work and I am sitting in a happy space. I am living a happier, healthier, more fulfilled life—and that spills out to everything around me, to my relationships, my work, everything. Healing and allowing yourself happiness and satisfaction in life can be a huge contribution to others because you have so much more to give. You're bringing more positivity to your world and raising the vibration of everything and everyone around you.

You can raise your vibration through dancing, laughing, or whatever else it is that makes you feel good. What will happen through healing is that you'll stay at a higher vibration almost all the time. I can have something bad happen to me and it doesn't have to faze me because I am in a place of gratitude and happiness. I understand that life happens, and you flow with it. The happier you are, the higher your vibration will go.

This all comes somewhere on the other side of healing—you'll learn to be in a happier, more joyful place—naturally. And when you're there, you'll start attracting better things into your life, and your connection to the Spirit world will be even stronger.

You can tell the difference in people who have done this work. It is in their presence: the light they bring into a room, and the energy they bring to a reading. There are some psychic mediums who tell you things in a negative light because that's the place they're in. They can't see and connect to the positive messages because they mostly see and respond to the negative ones. They are reflecting their own issues onto everybody else. They can even be doing harm because they can't help their sitters with healing. They can't bring the light of Spirit to their work. Their own unhappiness is hurting the people around them, just as ours can if we stay in a dark place and don't let any light into our lives. We can't offer what we don't have, so bringing peace and joy and positivity into our lives lets us give it freely to others. That's why I want to emphasize that your own healing, and your own happiness, are such important parts of your journey and your mediumship.

I am very cautious about sharing negative insights because my purpose is to facilitate healing and to raise vibration. Telling them negatives may not help them on their journey—so if I know something bad, I may choose not to say it unless I have clear communication from Spirit to do so. I want people to find their best path, their highest version of themselves and their lives. I do that with the aim of moving forward, and not pulling them back to old traumas or issues. Our lives are lived forward for a reason. All our vast potential lies in the future, so I try to help people look ahead, and make the next part of their unfolding a powerful and positive one.

However, I do ask if the sitter wants to know everything I am picking up. Infidelity may be one of those things. If I feel it, I will let the person know. When health concerns emerge, I will offer cautionary words and suggest seeking a medical check-up to confirm my impressions. Although you might deem these things as "negative," the intention is to give guidance that is loving or helpful. Bad news doesn't necessarily mean negative. It is life, right? Share challenging information with the clear intent to help the person and guide them. And, honestly, this has to be done on a case-by-case basis.

However, these following negative predictions or statements should be avoided at all times:

- predicting death/terminal illnesses
- invoking curses
- supporting beliefs of negative or evil spirits
- scaring people or invoking fear
- forecasting the loss of a baby/miscarriage
- indicating that Spirit is angry or carries negative emotions toward the sitter

Saying the things listed above has no value or positive purpose. It only causes fear and anxiety. In cases of life and death, humans are not the arbiter of these powerful transitions. We must stay humble and leave these occurrences to Source. Some things are just beyond the realm of human control and understanding. The mystery is always bigger than we are. What you can bring, however, is the greatest light possible to each reading—and this involves all the ways of caring for ourselves mentioned so far.

Caring for Your Body on This Journey

It is critical, therefore, that we care for our bodies. We tend to take our physical health for granted, but everything we currently experience, and every action we take, is through our material body.

The body is our soul's home here on Earth, and when we neglect it, everything else in our lives becomes harder. All the unhealthy habits you might have—a poor diet, a lack of adequate sleep, not exercising or moving in a positive manner—all of that affects your energy, attention, focus, sense of peace and well-being, and ultimately, your ability to connect to Spirit. So, take care of your body, listen to it, and respond to its needs. Practice keeping it vibrant and healthy, so it can help you do all the things that you want to accomplish.

As you're starting to work with Spirit and connecting to higher planes, the first thing I strongly suggest is to drink more water. And I do mean water—not sodas, coffee, or energy drinks, and certainly not sweetened beverages. Your body needs water. You're working with energy, and that will deplete you. Studies have shown that intense energy work can cause you to experience muscle cramps, exhaustion, and dehydration. Because you're sustaining a high vibrational energy, you want to make sure you're staying hydrated. Carry a water bottle with you, and before you start a practice, drink water. When you finish a session, drink more water. Get in the habit of staying hydrated. You can even use it as a centering activity and say an affirmation or a mantra when you drink. Take a deep breath or release tension—anything you can do to make the act of drinking water a positive part of your life and spiritual practice.

You may also want to eat lighter foods. This will come naturally. You will probably start getting away from eating as much red meat, and you'll start wanting to eat lighter because you are becoming a lighter being. That may mean staying clear of fast food, fried food, and processed foods in general. There are theories around meat, and what it does to your energy when you bring it into your body. Some mediums have gone to a vegetarian, or even a vegan, diet because they feel that it affects them or their readings. It is something you may want to start noticing: how you feel after a meal; if certain foods make you feel heavier in your body or more disconnected from Spirit; or if you have less energy. Of course, it is always up to you. I haven't given up meat completely. I still eat chicken and fish, but I have a really hard time eating beef these days. Don't do what everybody else is doing—do what's right for you and your body. You know your body better than anyone else.

Exercising and walking are other ways to help raise your vibration and help put you in a meditative state. I enjoy what I call *walking with purpose*. Every day, I try to do twenty minutes of meditating, twenty minutes of journaling, and then twenty minutes of walking. When you walk with purpose, you're raising your awareness. That's when you might see the red flowers, birds, and how colors change and become more vibrant, as you walk in an altered state. When I started meditating, that's what happened to me—colors became super vibrant. Everywhere I went, I felt that I was seeing things with different eyes. Walks are also great times to practice receiving messages from Spirit.

Walk with purpose, walk with an awareness, and notice everything around you. Don't walk and just look at your activity tracker or your phone. Don't think about some negative conversation or something that makes you angry. Instead, walk and notice every crack in the sidewalk, every flower, every cloud, every leaf, and particularly, notice their shapes. You'll see things in the shape of hearts—those are little messages of encouragement for you. Walking is a chance to clear your mind, raise your energy, connect to Spirit, and practice gratitude and love of life.

The Importance of Authenticity

On your journey, it is important to be authentic. Some people want to hide when they become a medium. They don't want to share certain insights or images out of fear of what people will think or say. They're afraid of judgment and ridicule and are reluctant to share their journey with a lot of people. Many mediums, when they first start, come up with another name because they don't want people to know who they really are.

Mediums often struggle with their religious upbringing, and it's sometimes difficult for them to explain why they are connecting to Spirit in this way. If they were raised Catholic or in other Christian denominations, it is beyond what those religions teach. I have friends who are now mediums, and their dads are preachers. They are struggling to reconcile their beliefs and abilities with their relationships. Sometimes it's difficult to bring all these pieces together in a positive way.

Becoming authentic will become an important part of your journey. You'll never be a great medium unless you can walk in your shoes honestly and be unafraid of who you are meant to be.

Remember, Spirit is there with you, and if you're working for Spirit, it is going to open doors for you. However, you still have to walk through the doors. That's what makes it so important to honor who you truly are.

Spirit asks us to be honest with ourselves and others, and our happiness is often dependent on how fully we can do this. Practice being honest and living authentically, and you'll find you ultimately become stronger, happier, and more connected to the other side. It may not be easy, but it is worth it, and Spirit will be with you every step of the way.

Triggers and Bringing Your Whole Self

As I mentioned before, if you want to be a medium, you have to work through your own traumas and let go of any negative or destructive beliefs and habits that you've acquired over time. You absolutely must do this because Spirit is going to bring you people who have had similar traumas as you, and if you haven't worked through those things yourself, you could get triggered. Then the session becomes more about you, and not the sitter.

That's one of the reasons why it is so important to heal yourself. It has to be a dual journey. You must be able to tell people your story, and you have to give them hope that everything can be okay. If you choose the path to do your healing work, then you will be more mindful when someone sits across from you who's been abused sexually or in other ways. You will not go "unconscious" and potentially narrow that channel that connects you to Spirit and the healing wisdom that you have acquired from your own life experience.

I have used the word "trigger" a number of times in this book, but what exactly does it mean to be triggered? How can it influence your ability to be a psychic? What might be a sign that you are triggered, and how might it affect your access to Spirit?

I'll give you an example. A lot of the trauma in my life is connected to men. Things that I experienced with men have made me more anxious or vulnerable in some ways. When a man books a reading with me, I feel sick the whole week beforehand. I have to ask myself why. I know I will still be able to connect to Spirit, so it is not about ability. But when I have to be vulnerable with a man, it brings up all these old fears. Why am I fearful? Why am I scared? Why am I starting to block myself? I am being triggered because I'm having to go into a vulnerable state and allow a man to be vulnerable with me, when I have a lack of trust in men. Men can also be more critical and non-believing, and that could be a part of it. However, I think a lot of it has to do with the trauma associated with the men in my life.

Those are deep-rooted issues that I am still working through. Spirit will guide me through these issues by sending me a lot of men for readings because that's what Spirit does. Spirit is going to give me lots of opportunities to overcome that anxiety and let go of those old feelings and beliefs. They're going to show me, over and over again, that it's all okay: I *can* do this. That's another reason why you want to work through your triggers. They can hurt your work and your ability to connect, but the longer they stay around, the more unhappiness they will bring you.

Everything ultimately comes down to the same thing.

You may have something completely different: it could be a relationship with a parent; it could be a loss; it could be something about yourself that you're insecure about. Your response to a trigger could be feeling overwhelmed, crying, or getting angry and lashing out. It could be that you get controlling, in some situations. Whatever your response to the trigger is, it pulls you from a state of calm or happiness into an "unconscious" automatic response—this negative place. You are carrying this wound around with you, and every time you meet someone who touches it, even accidentally, you're feeling the original pain all over again. You can't bring your best to Spirit, the sitter, or yourself, when you're in pain. You just can't.

You have to let go of those traumas and overcome your triggers. Meditation, journaling, and the other things I mentioned earlier, can be very helpful with this. It's possible that you might need therapy. It doesn't matter how you get there; you need to do whatever it takes to heal and let go. You need to move into your happiest and best version of yourself and your life.

Spirit Guides and Accepting the Unknown

You are not alone in this journey. We all have a team of spirit guides, some of whom have been with us since birth. The purpose of this team is to guide you through your human experience here on Earth. Spirit guides are those who were once human themselves and have attained a higher level of spiritual mastery.

Learning about spirit guides is another important step in your spiritual journey. The idea of spirit guides comes from Western Spiritualism, as do many of the other tools in this book. Whether the idea resonates with you and you adopt the belief is totally up to you. But learning about and connecting to your guides can give your inner spiritual voice a name. It can help you trust that inner voice. So much of what we do with Spirit comes down to learning to trust, accept, and be open to messages and truths that we receive.

It is hugely beneficial to know that we don't do this work or walk this path alone. Someone is beside us, rooting for us, and helping us, every step along the way. Knowing that someone who cares is at your side can calm you in difficult times and inspire you to reach for greater heights. That's true of the people in your life, and it is one of the roles of your spirit guides as well. Reach out and start learning to connect directly with them. Let them help you as much as they can. Becoming a medium is not an easy calling, so it is good to have that extra support, that team, to help you on your path.

The concept of spirit guides in Western Spiritualism originated from the nineteenth-century Spiritualist movement. Leaders in this movement had mediumistic capabilities. They believed that they made contact with angels, or highly evolved beings, who gave them great wisdom. According to theological doctrine, spirit guides are not always of human descent. Some live as energy or light beings in the cosmic realm. Some guides are people who have lived many former lifetimes and paid their karmic debts, and they have advanced beyond the need to reincarnate. Spirit guides have always been a part of Native American spirituality. Many Native American traditions required taking strenuous vision quests that required lengthy periods of fasting and movement deprivation, all designed to get them in touch with the Spirit world. The knowledge of spirit guides, or something similar, is an old belief in many different cultures.

You have major guides who are with you throughout your entire lifetime who will help you learn life's lessons. You will also have minor guides who come into your life temporarily and help you with issues at any given time.

Characteristics of spirit guides include a non-judgmental perspective. They are aware of your difficulties and offer guidance. You can have multiple spiritual guides, and that number can fluctuate depending on what Spirit deems is needed in your life at the time.

Individuals rarely see spirit guides with their physical eyes. Mostly a spirit guide's presence is sensed or seen with one's *inner vision*. Identifying their presence can be done by feeling a slight pressure on the head, arms, or back of the neck. Sudden chills or goosebumps that occur when thinking about a particular issue is a sign that your spirit guide is with you. A slight jerk of the body, similar to what we sometimes experience when falling asleep, can be a sign that a spirit guide is with you. A buzzing sound frequency might be a signal that the spirit guide wants to be noticed. Seeing any little twinkling lights in the room can also be a spirit guide. There are all kinds of little cues, and they can vary based on which guide is nearby. You can learn to identify their presence through the sounds or sensations that they bring with them.

Spirit guides help us in many unseen ways throughout our lives, usually without our knowing. But as psychics, we can learn to communicate more directly. Guides can contact us through our dreams, in meditations, through synchronicities, automatic writing, the use of pendulums, or scrying (gazing into a black mirror). The practice of bibliomancy, gaining spiritual insight by opening a book to a random place to get insight, is another way. Visualizations, plant medicine dreams, trances, immersion into nature, and meditative art are all different ways of connecting to your guides and making yourself open to their wisdom.

In the very beginning of my journey—and this will be similar to almost everybody's journey—I was introduced to the idea of spirit guides, and I wanted, more than anything in the world, to know who these beings were for me. You'll want to meditate to find out more about them, learn their names, and discover what lives they've lived. It's just the way we function as humans, at this point, because we haven't been far enough in our journey to just surrender and trust.

The human part of us needs answers. We want to know names. We want to know what lifetime our guides came from. Why are they here? What are they doing? You'll want to create a story about them and yourself. I was overcome with curiosity at the idea of having invisible helpers at my side and knowing that there were entities helping me navigate my life, loving me, and looking out for me, through everything.

I would like to share something that I wish I had understood from the beginning. Learn to surrender—don't worry so much about the details of who your guides are—and you'll have a much better experience. To be honest, in the spirit realm, if you've lived many lifetimes, what name would you want them to call you? Which life would you choose it from? Even though names are very significant to humans, we are not our name. So really, names don't matter. At the end of the day, it's not about what their name is, or what past lifetime you shared together.

You can call your guides by anything you want—any name that serves you. When I started this journey, I kept seeing the name Marcus everywhere. I assigned that name to my main guide; I call him Marcus. It doesn't matter, Spirit isn't going to take offense at the name you choose. The important thing isn't who they were, or what name someone once called them. Their role in your life is as a helper, a hand on your shoulder, or a gentle nudge in the right direction.

Your goal with your guides is to learn from them and receive guidance and comfort from them. Focus on what they are offering you and open yourself up to their wisdom and power. It's good to be able to call on different guides or different energies, depending on what you're dealing with in your life, and on what you need at that moment. It can be useful to recognize which guide you're addressing, but it is all for your benefit.

Through channeling classes and meditative practices, I have determined that I have a guide that paces. I could feel him striding back and forth, so I call him my Protector. I don't know who he is, and I don't need a name for him. I just call him my Protector, and he's the one I visualize. He keeps anything negative away from me. His job is to be my gatekeeper, and that's just what he does. Your understanding of a guide can be determined by their role in your life.

Along my journey, I was trying to find the woman who I am and empower myself because of all the trauma that I had experienced. One time during meditation, I felt this divine feminine energy from up high, but I didn't see her physically—it was more of a knowing. I call her Mary. Now she's the guide that I tap into when I need to feel my feminine side.

My advice to you about your guides is to play with them, meditate, do whatever you want to do, but don't get hung up on who they are or what their names are. There are some philosophies that believe a guide can be half man, half animal. Your guides might be mermaids, sphinxes, fairies, centaurs, or fauns. One thing I love about Spiritualism is that it's not a box that follows convention and dictates, "This is the way it has to be." I think Spiritualism is really about creating your own reality of things. Along my journey, some people told me that there's no way my dad could be a spirit guide because a spirit guide lives multiple lives. That may feel true for them, but it doesn't feel true to me. There are no rules when it comes to connecting with our guides.

Loved ones who pass on may care about us, watch over us, and help guide us. Whether you consider that to fit your definition of a spirit guide, or is just a Spirit who is providing guidance, doesn't matter. Don't get hung up on someone else's rules, because we can't know for certain the whole truth of the afterlife from this life's perspective.

Look for that which *feels* true and helps you on your journey. I know that my dad is around, and I know that he helps guide me, so I call on him. He acts as one of my guides. I think that's just the uniqueness of spirituality. We can take what fits and resonates with us and create our own religion out of it. We are shaping our own belief system from what we learn along the way and the things that resonate for us. We can feel truth and meaning when we find them, and we react to them on a deep level. We can look at all these different ideas and possibilities and choose which ones are right for us.

Some people will use animal totems as their guides because they feel a strong connection to the animal. During one channeling experience, I had a teacher who asked us to go into a meditation and find an animal, because we can always tap into the energy of that animal to gain strength. As you go along on your journey, you'll discover that your animals will change as you grow in your spiritual connection.

You could be a bear at this point in your life, if you need to be a bear. Personally, I was a mama bear at one point in my life; I was still protecting my cubs. I had some problems with one of my kids getting into trouble, so I really needed that power. I was also raising a teenage boy. So, for me, channeling that mama bear energy helped me out a lot.

People also think of ancestors; your great ancestors can also be guides. If you're interested in herbs, for example, maybe that interest came from your ancestors, and it keeps getting passed down through the generations. A lot of people are attracted to the Native American culture but aren't Native American. However, they might have ancestors from Native American culture that are their guides.

Our connections might be from past lives. There could be a lot of reasons for a connection, but if it resonates for you, lean into that, embrace it, and see where it takes you. I can imagine having a Native American leader as one of my guides too. There is so much wisdom available and so much to learn from Native cultures. Let the connection flow, surrender to it, trust that your guides are there, and I promise you that you'll have a better experience.

Light beings and guardian angels can be considered guides. Plants, as well as animals, can be guides. Shamanism believes that plants are energy and contain guidance. Some people believe in gods, goddesses, and ascended masters—beings that have already lived on this Earth and have elevated past the cycle of incarnation.

Earlier, I talked about how important imagination is to psychic work and mediumship, and to just trust it. Remember that whole right-brain/left-brain thing? When your imagination is working, that is often Spirit giving you inspiration. It's the left brain that's saying, "Oh, that's just your imagination."

So again, the big word is *trust*. And that's the hardest thing to master. If you don't trust in your real life, you're not going to trust in your spiritual life. Your guides and Spirit can use your imagination as a means of connecting to you. They can plant ideas and possibilities for you through your imagination. Imagination is a tool of Spirit and can be used to connect to information and experiences that are not directly our own. Let the imagination flow and just believe in it, and then you'll have the most amazing experiences possible.

Exercises and Methods to Connect with Your Guides

Here are a few exercises that will help you connect with your guides. With each one, remember that all answers and insights are coming through you and where you are. Spirit is never wrong, but we sometimes get in the way, or we bring our pain and trauma with us, and that affects what we receive. Always judge the information you receive in light of what is best for you and what helps you on your journey. Remember: Spirit, and especially your guides, are here to help you, so look for love and insight as a sign you're receiving clearly. Pay special attention to what feels right, and keep in mind what Spirit is trying to tell you. When you are done with an exercise, thank Spirit for its help, and sit for a few moments with how you feel and what you learned, or write in your journal about your experience.

Setting the Intention with a Prayer

First, we're going to set the intention. Here is an invocation I use:

"Today, we set the intention to work with our spirit guides. We open this space to the energies of the divine source and ask that these energies keep us safe. We invite only those of the highest vibration to connect with our hearts and provide us with information for our best and highest good."

If you feel drawn to it, you can also create your own intention. An intention is a guiding principle for how you want to live and show up in the world. An intention prayer should be a clear and specific wish you would like to align your thoughts and attitude to your guides. It can be as simple as a word or phrase. To set your own intention prayer, consider the following:

- Be direct.
- Be specific.
- Keep it positive.
- Come from the heart.
- Evoke feeling and purpose.

You can always create new intention prayers as your understanding grows and you start connecting to Spirit on a deeper level. You can create different phrases for different actions. Simply repeat the same phrase each time the act is performed. Before every reading, I ask the guides, angels, and ancestors to come through with specific evidence that my sitter will understand. I ask that the messages provide nothing but healing, compassion, and love. And so it is. You can do this type of intention for almost anything you do. As always, follow where the Universe is leading you and trust what feels right.

Here's an exercise on how to feel your guides. Find a quiet space to sit and relax. Close your eyes and take four cleansing breaths. Say your prayer of intention and invite your guides to come close to you. In your mind, request that they get even closer to you. Ask for them to allow you to feel their presence, and then hold space for them. Once you start to feel them, be sure to thank them, and then respectfully ask them to leave the room.

As they depart, notice the difference in energy in the room. You should be able to distinguish the difference with practice.

Document the feelings you got when they were near. Did you have any tingles on your body? Make note. This could be their calling card for you.

Meditation is also a great way to find your guides. One of my favorite meditations for this is by Gordon Smith, called "Meet Your Guides Meditation," and it may be found on YouTube.

Automatic Writing

Automatic writing is another exercise that you can practice. Find a quiet space where you can be alone. Say your intention prayer. Set a timer for ten minutes. Take three deep, cleansing breaths, and then just start writing whatever comes to you. Once the timer goes off, go back and read what you wrote, and analyze it to discover what the words mean to you. See if there are any clues or messages that you can decipher. Be open to whatever comes and thank your guides for their help.

Remember to ask and look only for positive messages that help you on your journey. If you find negativity or dark thoughts in your writing, they are most likely coming through from your past trauma, and they can be set aside. You are the channel that all messages are coming through, so if you're still working through your own issues, that may affect what you receive. Your guides are here to help you and lift you up towards your bright future and best self. Writing can bring out a lot of different ideas, and they may not all make sense or be useful at this time. Learn to find the nuggets of wisdom and truth that may be within.

Pendulums

Pendulum work is also a tool for connecting with Spirit. A pendulum board is a divination tool that is used in conjunction with a pendulum. It can help you acquire spiritual direction, guidance, and answers from your guides or loved ones in Spirit. A pendulum board can be made of wood, cardboard, paper, or cloth. You can even print one on paper. There are several types that you can find. Most will have the words "yes," "no," and "maybe" printed on them. Some will also have numbers and letters.

Always keep your pendulum clean by using sound vibrations, cleaning crystals, salt, incense, or moonwater. (Create moonwater by placing a bowl of water on your windowsill or porch so it can "absorb" the energy of moonlight while you sleep. This is said to have a purifying effect.)

Before you start with the pendulum exercise, write down questions that you have been hoping to have answered. They should be "yes" or "no" questions to begin with. Say your intention prayer. Hold your pendulum chain in your hand between your thumb and index finger and suspend it over the board. You can use either hand.

At first, the pendulum will appear to move all on its own. If you are not using a board and just want to ask yes/no questions, you will need to establish which direction is "yes" and which is "no." You can do this by asking the pendulum to show you a "no" and then a "yes." Once you have established your signs for yes and no, you can begin to ask the pendulum yes/no questions. If you are using a board, you can ask yes/no questions and see where the pendulum moves on the board. You can also ask for numbers or letters that are on your pendulum board and see where the pendulum moves. Ask your guides for guidance on each question. Be specific in your inquiries. Document the answers you receive.

Bibliomancy and Angel Cards

Bibliomancy is another way that you can communicate with your spirit guides. Select a book that you will use for this exercise. It can be any book, but I would suggest you use a self-help book. You can even use The Bible for this exercise. I want you to sit, calm your mind, and take three deep breaths. Set your intention and say your intention phrase. Close your eyes and let your fingers wander through the book pages. When it feels right, stop and make note of what page your fingers land on. Read the paragraph or the page that you landed on. Apply the wisdom.

You can also do this with angel cards. You can get a deck of angel cards, lay them out, and feel the energy over them. Then let your finger be drawn to a specific one. Pick the card that you feel drawn to, flip it over to read the message, and apply that to your life or question. Always keep in mind that when you are asking for help and guidance, it is important to apply what you receive. Sometimes part of the lesson or insight is only understood when you take action. One step forward often leads to something else that Spirit has in store.

Nature Immersion

Nature immersion is another exercise that you can do as well. When you take the time to look and pay attention, nature is subliminally magical. It is also a beautiful place to come into contact with your guides—especially animal Spirits and trans-species beings, also known as fairies. I don't experience a connection to these beings personally, but many people do. Discover what is true for you and how your guides present themselves. Nature is a wonderful place to connect to Spirits of all kinds, and natural places have a long history of being used for Spirit work. You may find yourself more open, or more at peace, in nature, which aids the work as well.

To practice nature immersion, find someplace outside—sit in a park, by a river or a stream, or go hiking. Look at the clouds, the bodies of water, and the trees. Do you get any glimpses of faces? What animals keep appearing near you while you are walking? Be aware of all your surroundings. Allow your mind to wander across the land, or deep within the plants, or down into the soil. See if any thoughts or insights come unbidden. You can meditate or practice a walking meditation as well. Imagine yourself being one with this place, with the plants and animals that live there, or imagine the area throughout time. Be open to any and all messages that you may receive.

Scrying

The last one is scrying. Now this is probably a less conventional way of meeting your guides. Scrying is just another divination tool, but its history traces back to Ancient Greece and the Oracles of Delphi. The first step is to create a completely darkened room and use only a candle for light. The darkened room is modeled after the completely pitch-black underground chambers of the oracles.

In this modern-day version, use a clear piece of glass, such as one from a photo frame. Use a black paint and paint the back of the glass in the frame. Hold the glass up to the light after dry to make sure all spaces are filled completely. Do another coat if necessary. Since you are painting the back, the front still has the shiny glass surface that allows for a reflection.

Once you've got your space, reflective surface, and candles, you're set to go. Get comfortable, take a deep breath and let it out, clear your mind, and focus on what you're about to do. Create your intent and ask your questions—aloud or to yourself. Visualize your question and then imagine you are pushing the image(s) out into the world. Your intent can be anything—but it should be crystal clear.

Begin by looking at the surface of the mirror. At one point, it may go black or silvery, and you will feel a shift. You're on the way. People describe that the reflective surface itself becomes much like water. Allow it to move and change, then ask your questions, or state your intent again.

If you are looking into the glass with little light (the room should be as dark as possible with only your candle for light), you may be able to see patterns, symbols, pictures, images, faces, or words forming in the reflective surface. You can do the same thing with water or any reflective surface.

Find the Tools that Work for You

Of all these methods, I use meditation most frequently because, in my experience, it is the best tool for connecting. I also nature-walk almost every day, and deeply listen to my own guides and departed loved ones while I walk. In my own practice, I use pendulums to help with the yes/no questions that my clients have. These have been the most reliable for me. I encourage you to try any of the tools of connection that call to you and find the methods that work best. You'll probably find, as I have, that a combination of techniques yields the most effective results. As always, trust Spirit and yourself. Find your path forward with your guides at your side.

CHAPTER SEVEN

HOW SPIRIT SPEAKS

It is love's soft breath on life's dark coals that briefly reds the fire.
-John Holland

On your journey, you will start with yourself and work outward. By now, you should be practicing your meditation, journaling, and affirmations, and doing the work necessary to move on from any trauma you may have experienced in the past. Then you can focus on raising your vibration, connecting to your guides, and learning to tap into the power and potential that you inherently possess.

Now we start opening up to the miraculous possibilities that come with stepping into true mediumship. True mediumship means receiving communication directly from those who have passed on, and acting as an intermediary for the Spirit realm. And to do that, you have to learn the language of Spirit.

Talking to Spirit is not like having a conversation with someone in this life. Spirit doesn't typically speak in full sentences, as we do in our conversations; we don't usually see Spirits with our eyes or hear them with our ears. They give us pictures in our mind's eye or create a thought or word in our brain. They connect to our feelings and senses and draw our eyes to something we can see or play a song that contains meaning in the words. They speak to us through synchronicities and signs. We sense their presence and learn over time how to interpret what they give us. A medium knows how to translate these bits and pieces into a meaningful narrative for the sitter. The art of mediumship is about learning and becoming aware of the subtleties, and then, interpreting their meaning.

I don't know why Spirit works this way, but I do know that we have to work within the framework Spirit gives us and learn to uncover the meaning. We must understand it personally before we can translate it for someone else. This was one of the big lessons for me, discovering how much of what we learn from Spirit comes to us through our mind and needs interpretation. Often, it is closer to imagination than it is to conversation.

Spirit uses our brain, body, and all of our senses to connect. These senses are referred to as "the clairs." Spirit triggers these clairs, or senses, in the communication process. Before I understood how mediumship works, I assumed mediums actually saw people in front of them. When mediums said, "I see . . . ," I thought that they really saw something. When they said, "Oh, I hear Spirit telling me . . . ," I thought that they really heard Spirit. However, that is almost never the case. Usually, everything happens within the brain of our own central nervous system. Now I am not saying that actual seeing and hearing never happens. We all work differently, but most of the time, it is internal. Understanding that will help alleviate frustration and your need to compare yourself to how others receive information.

There are many ways to practice clairs. Part of developing your clair senses is simply by developing your senses in general. When you pay attention to what you see, hear, smell, or taste, and tune into your physical or emotional sensations, you will be able to recognize and decode Spirit communications with more confidence. You can be of greater assistance to a sitter if you are specific: "I am smelling apple cider," rather than, "I am smelling something spiced or fruity."

Details can make a big difference. Therefore, some of the following exercises are about expanding your ability to pay attention and offer specifics, to notice and remember more, so you can pass along as much detail as possible.

The Brain and The Clairs

Before we can fully understand the clairs, we first need a very basic introduction to the brain and how we process information. I learned these foundational ideas from psychic medium Lisa Williams at a weekend mentorship in Lily Dale, a community of mediums in upstate New York. Lisa drew a picture of a brain for us, explaining the various regions—left brain, right brain, "gator brain," cerebral cortex—and the roles they play in our readings. Lisa explained that when we process information, the various parts of the brain process it differently:

- The cerebral cortex is the part of the brain that manages sight, hearing, smell, and sensation. This is the part of the brain that Spirit uses to leave impressions or communicate with us.

- The right brain refers to areas in our brain that are engaged in creative and metaphoric processes—and where Spirit gives us impressions through our imagination. Imagination is key in mediumship. You must have an open mind, or you will receive and interpret limiting information.
- The left brain is the term used to refer to the regions of our brain where we process information analytically and literally. The left brain is always analyzing and checking for literal and rationally known information and often doubts information that is more intuitive.
- The limbic brain floods us with emotion. Learning to control emotions in a mediumship reading is also key. If you get emotional, then it puts the focus on you, and the reading should never be about you.
- The "gator brain," or amygdala, is the control center of our fight-or-flight response and can create panic when we get something wrong. It gives us an anxious feeling, but it's also the part of the brain that tries to connect the dots and make sense of random information. This is a kind of survival mechanism: when we are presented with disparate facts or impressions, we try to make sense of them, in part, to be sure we are not in danger. When the mind becomes confused, the tendency is to want to make sense of things quickly.

Your objective as a medium is to lean into each piece of information without intrusion of the more analytical, emotional, or anxious parts of your psyche. The more relaxed and open you are, the better you will receive the intended meanings of Spirit. For example, let's say I receive these four pieces of information in a reading:

- mom
- alcohol
- car
- sapphire

Early in my development as a medium, my brain would rush in to fill in the gaps:

"Your mom died in a car accident involving alcohol, and the color of the car was sapphire."

A seasoned medium, on the other hand, feels into each item, and fully explores the significance individually. Essentially, with experience, a medium slows down the automatic analytical and emotional processes that jump to create making meaning right away. A veteran medium knows to go little by little.

Since the right brain is our intuition and imagination, work on surrendering. Since the left brain is the chatter brain and tells us "This can't be right," you need to meditate to control it. Meditation also offers us the centeredness that can moderate emotions and cultivate calmness. Trust the information you receive, and don't panic if you are wrong. Don't fill in the blanks. Cultivate the gifts of the right brain through meditation, sitting in your power, and clearing your own emotional field.

So, if I received the image or word "alcohol," I might first assume it was the Spirit who had the issue. But if I sit with "alcohol" and lean into it, feel into it, ask for clarity, suddenly my awareness is expanded. It is a kind of unfolding that only becomes possible when the medium becomes more available to the right brain's way of processing information.

In this example, I was able to offer the sitter an accurate reading by going through each discrete image and exploring it deeply, mindfully.

- mom – "I have your mom here."
- alcohol – "She tells me you are struggling with alcohol."
- car – "She also says that you have her car now."
- sapphire – "She also tells me that her sapphire ring was passed down to a family member."

Understanding how the brain works will help you in your mediumship journey. Explore how and why you process things a certain way, or why you interpret things the way you do. Why do you get scared and want to run out of the room sometimes? That will happen. You're going to panic when you feel like you're not getting anything, or you are getting nos. You're going to get sweaty and nervous, and that's when the "gator" brain's fight-or-flight mechanism will kick in.

Your left brain and your right brain will be in constant battle in the early stages of your development. Your left brain will tell you that you are making everything up. Your left brain will pick apart and try to overanalyze every thought, feeling, and intuition you receive. In the beginning, you will want to meditate for an hour before every single reading you do. Why? Because that is the

You Can Be a Medium

only time you will trust the information. The information comes to you when the left brain is quiet. Eventually, you will develop your feelings and know when thoughts are not your own, without having to meditate beforehand. It comes with practice. If you have knowledge and understanding, then you have an awareness of how it could affect your mediumship, and how to work on it.

Clairvoyance

We will start with clairvoyance, which means "clear seeing." Clairvoyance can be visions you have during meditation or sleep, a quick flash of a picture in your mind's eye, or even something external that attracts your attention.

You could be in the middle of a reading and be drawn to an item in the room you are in, such as a picture or a painting, for example. During one reading, I kept looking at a picture on my wall of me, walking across a rope bridge in Ireland. I asked my sitter, "Did your grandfather live near a bridge?"

And the sitter said, "Yes, how did you know that?"

I replied, "Well, because Spirit showed me."

Learn to trust your awareness and ask yourself: Why am I looking at that? Why is my gaze pulled this way?

One time, right before doing a reading, I saw birds on the tree outside my window. For some reason, they caught my attention. "Is there something here that I am meant to see?" I thought to myself.

About ten minutes later, I did a reading with a woman whose best friend had recently died of cancer. This woman had spent a lot of time sitting with her dying friend. One day, they were looking out the window and were startled by the sight of a bird falling out of the tree, as though it had suddenly been struck dead. They would share that story frequently over the time that her friend had left. That occurrence is a perfect example of external clairvoyance, where you see something with your physical eyes, and then your internal clairvoyance creates the images that come into your mind as something seen with the inner eye.

One beautiful fall day, I was at the park with my grandkids. I snapped a really cute picture of my grandson. It captured the essence of who he is very well, and I sent it to his mom, my daughter. A few weeks later, I got invited to be a speaker at a local psychic conference. I was excited to take part and accepted the invitation. I would have an hour-and-a-half to speak on the topic of my choice. Since this was my first time participating as a speaker, I wanted to choose a subject that wasn't spoken about frequently. I started looking through my journals and class notes from the last three years, to get some inspiration.

I finally came up with an idea. I loved the topic so much that not only could I speak about it, but I could also develop a class on it. I could possibly even write a book on it. I felt the momentum very strongly: I was being called to do it. I began brainstorming and outlining my ideas. While flipping through my journals, I was reminded of a concept that I had for the cover of a book that I wanted to write one day. This journal entry was from a year-and-a-half earlier. It was a doodle of a little girl holding a teddy bear in front of a brick wall. Behind the wall was a heart. I knew that I would have to find someone to illustrate my concept once I had a home for it. This concept would be perfect for my class idea. It was time to manifest this vision into reality.

While I was working on my class, I decided to take a break and check social media. Scrolling through Instagram, I saw that my daughter posted a picture of my grandson, the one I took in the park, as well as a drawing of the same photo. A resident at the apartment complex she works at had made a sketch of it for her. I was immediately drawn to her work. Maybe she could bring my concept to life?

I reached out to my daughter to see if her acquaintance would do a commissioned piece for me. I have friends who are artists and could have done this for me easily, but Spirit had other plans in mind, and was pulling me in another direction. I sent my daughter a message, explaining exactly what I wanted, with a picture from my journal entry. She agreed to reach out to the artist and would let me know.

The following day, I got two urgent calls and a text message from my daughter. She said that I had to call her back as soon as possible. She proceeded to tell me that she spoke with the artist about my idea. The woman was a little taken back at first and explained to my daughter that she had drawn that very concept five years ago. She said that sometimes she gets ideas and "knows" that they will manifest into something one day. She went back to her apartment to see if she could find the artwork that she had done. She brought back a drawing that was exactly what I had described. My own drawing and this one was nearly identical in what they showed. The girl with a limp teddy bear hanging from her right hand, the dress, the heart behind the wall, even the placement of the wall, were all the same. It was dated almost exactly five years ago, to the day.

I spent most of the night trying to logically explain how this could happen. I was being pulled by my logical mind, rather than accepting the meaning that Spirit was offering. Maybe I had seen this image before and stored it in my subconscious mind. I scoured the internet trying to find this image somewhere, but I turned up nothing. Even if it was not original, how could I explain the series of events that led me to reach out to a person I had never met, to create a concept that she had created five years ago? The only explanation is that there is some kind of master plan that is in place. All things happen for a reason. Ultimately, we are all one. You must surrender, trust, and believe that the inspiration you are given is coming from a higher place. I received validation in a really big way that I was meant to create and develop the idea. I needed to use the inspiration that was given to me. Apparently, the time had come—perfect, divine timing.

Clairvoyance is one of the most common ways of receiving communication, whether through seeing things in the mind's eye, having certain images or items show up repeatedly, or having your eyes drawn to something that you're supposed to see. It takes time to learn what different images or symbols mean to you and how to lead clients through the information that you're getting to find out how it ties into their loved one or their story. As with all mediumship work, practice and patience are key. Once you start understanding the visual language that Spirit is using, you will open up all kinds of messages, and more and more specific communications.

Clairvoyance Exercises
Practice One: Matching Game

Do you recall playing Old Maid when you were a child? You can buy this deck at most toy stores. The deck contains images of all kinds with duplicates of each picture. A player throws the cards on the floor, randomly, and face up. The player looks at all of them, even imagining taking a mental snapshot to remember where each card is placed. Then the person turns all the cards face down and attempts to recall where the matching cards are.

Buy a deck, get a timer, and see how fast you can remember where things are, with the aim of increasing your ability to visualize what and where cards are.

Practice Two: Item Recall

Another exercise is to memorize the contents of a friend's purse or glove compartment. Take one minute to look at everything in the purse or glove compartment, and then put everything back. List all the items you can recall and see how many you get right.

All Kinds of Memory Games

There are books full of memory games, and you can find memory games online too. These activities cultivate your ability to be observant and notice everything. This is one of the most important skills you can possibly develop; psychic mediums need crystal-clear perception.

Notice details; notice everything. Practice when you're walking with purpose—look at what makes each yard unique, and notice what signs you see. Learning to go deeper when looking at life will help you see deeper with Spirit. Look closer, learn to really see, and be open to signs wherever you go. This will strengthen your connection to the other side—and with your sitters. As a result of developing these skills, you will be able to offer more specifics in your readings and bring more Spirit to life.

Clairaudience

The next clair is clairaudience—"clear hearing." Clear hearing can help you get names, communicate with your higher self, and get guidance from Spirit.

Clairaudience can happen both internally in your brain, and externally, where you hear words or sounds near you. Before my journey started, I was hearing my name being called by Spirit in my house. This is an example of external hearing. Mostly, the hearing you will receive will be internal hearing, in the form of thoughts. When you are getting a thought in your own voice, and you know it's not your idea, that's clairaudience.

External clairaudience refers to external sounds that draw one's attention. If you are doing a reading, and all of a sudden birds are chirping right outside your window, and you notice and can't shake the sound of them, then they might have a meaning for your Spirit or sitter. Clairaudience can also be music. Spirit often uses music to communicate. Music might either play inside your head, or you might hear a song on your tablet or phone right before a reading and know it has meaning.

I have never been a diehard fan of Stevie Nicks, although I did grow up listening to her and even owned an album back in the day. But a Stevie Nicks song gave me another lesson in paying attention to synchronicities, to seeing and following the breadcrumbs that Spirit leaves for us.

I had been in Houston on business. I was settled in for the night, when I got a text from a lady that I have been practicing on to refine my gift. I am going to refer to her as "Love Story." She asked to schedule another meeting with me. I was very apprehensive because I had a successful reading in the past with her, but just wasn't sure that I could recreate the magic. Reluctantly, I agreed to meet her in a few days. I was a little stressed out about it. What if I disappointed her? This trusting-Spirit thing is a little nerve-wracking!

I went on about my evening, flipping through channels. I ended up on the season premiere of *The Voice*. My attention was caught by a cover version of the song "Landslide," by Stevie Nicks. "What a great song!" I thought to myself.

Thursday morning, I woke up with feelings I often have when I am tapping into Spirit, and thoughts were flashing through my head. I saw a set of initials, internally heard the words, "It is my birthday," and song lyrics: *"If you see my reflection in the snow-covered hills . . . ."* Yep, lyrics from Stevie Nicks' "Landslide."

Then I got the strong feeling that Love Story was not doing well, and probably needed to hear from me, so I reached out to her and gave her the information that I had gotten that morning. The initials were hers, based on her maiden name—which I didn't know. The birthday belonged to her soul mate, who had passed away some time ago. His birthday was coming up. She could not, however, place "Landslide" as significant. By then, *I knew* that Spirit is never wrong! I knew that there had to be something with that song. Maybe it was a message for me?

Stevie Nicks wrote that song in Colorado at one of the lowest points in her life. Love Story had just returned from Colorado. Remember, I got this overwhelming *feeling* that she was not doing well? Maybe that was it.

In the months before this, Spirit had made themselves known to me through dimes. I was finding dimes all over my house, in the most random places. They were Spirit's current calling card to me, so I had my eyes peeled for dimes. If I were to find one, that would mean I was on the right track, a little thumbs up from the Spirit world. But there was nothing; I would just have to wait. One night I was getting ready for bed and started to scroll through Facebook. Out of nowhere, a post from an old high school classmate of mine came across my feed. It went something like this: "My old high school crush Stevie Nicks is going to be on *The Late Late Show* tonight!" Ha, okay, Spirit, I get it! I am on the right track!

Friday morning comes around. I meditate for a short time to get prepared for my reading. I just can't get this Stevie Nicks thing out of my mind. There must be more to this! I just know it in my gut. I decided that I need to find out what she sang on *The Late Late Show*. If it was "Landslide," then I would know I was getting closer to an answer! I searched and searched, and was about to give up, when I stumbled across the performance, just freshly posted, on YouTube. I anxiously clicked it open to listen. To my disappointment, it was not "Landslide." I felt deflated. I was just hours away from my meeting. This all had to mean something!

Reluctantly, I decided to listen to the song she sang. *Stevie Nicks sang "Leather and Lace."* This was the song I was meant to hear! This is where Spirit was leading me. This was Love Story's love story! Everything fit! The song is about a couple that didn't seem to match, an incongruent love. My client had been in a bad marriage at the time, and the person she fell in love with was an officer. Her husband at the time was in the service as well. The strong soul connection was there; the love story was there. But careers and lives could have been damaged. They were never able to act upon their love, and then her soul mate passed away. When I heard this song, I felt as if he were singing it to her. It moved me tremendously, and I knew it was what she needed to hear. It was what I'd been led to find by Spirit.

I went to pull the original from her *Belladonna* album, which was the same album that I owned as a kid. The original was a duet with Don Henley, and when Don came on it was as though Love Story's soul mate had a voice again! It sounded as if he was speaking directly to her. I just knew that this was what it was all about!

While I was making my bed, before leaving for my appointment with her, there it was. The sign from Spirit that I was on the right track: In the middle of my bed, under the blankets, was a single dime. I literally cried. I was about to give this lady the most incredible experience. Her session was not about proving that there is life after death or that I was actually communicating with her loved one. We had already established all those things in earlier sessions. This session was about *feelings*. This was giving Spirit a voice again, to convey his *feelings* toward her. That day, she was going to hear and feel her soul mate again.

We always meet in a central location between our homes, usually a study room or a library. When she arrived, I had her sit down and asked her to let me take her on a journey of my week, and all the events that had led us to this moment. Then I handed her the lyrics of "Leather and Lace" that I had printed out and played the song for her. When the words, *"I search only for something I can't see"* played, tears started falling from her eyes. As the song played on, and Don Henley's part played, she literally gasped, and more tears came down. I have to say that it was the most beautiful experience I had ever witnessed.

When it was all over, she looked over at me in utter amazement and just said, "Thank you." She let me know that before our meeting, she was angry at her soul mate. She had been asking him to just let her know how he felt, since their love here on Earth was unrequited. She had never known for certain if he felt for her what she felt for him. Spirit made it clear that day that love transcends. I know there are skeptics out there that might think that this was all a coincidence. Trust me, I second-guessed myself for a whole day afterwards. Was it really as magical as I had experienced? Yes, it was! Two days later, Love Story sent me a text. She is an avid reader and had just picked up a new book to read. A couple of chapters into the novel, the couple in the story decide to go out on a date, and they end up at their local pub named . . . **Leather and Lace.**

All these remarkable synchronicities revolved around one song—and clairaudience.

Clairaudience Exercise: Tuning In

Play one of your favorite songs, and while you're sitting there, with your eyes closed, pick out one instrument that you hear, and then zero in on that one instrument. Do that for a minute and then switch your focus to a different instrument for a minute. Train your ears to hear subtle differences and to focus in on details.

You can even do this just sitting in your home by listening to the sounds in your home; and then go outside and imagine yourself walking there. What are you hearing? Stretch your ears even further. Building up your clairs is like building up your muscles.

Another place you can use to develop clairaudience is in your imagination. Spend some time in silence, and then start to imagine sounds, one at a time. Hear and feel each one—a baby crying, rain hitting a tin roof, a dog barking, someone talking with an accent, a phone ringing, a door slamming, a knock on the door, or car tires screeching. This will train you to hear in your mind's ear.

Clairsentience

Clairsentience is "clear feeling." It is physical and emotional. This clair helps with identifying relationships, physical attributes, emotions, personality, illnesses, and even cause of death. Determining the relationship between Spirit and the sitter can sometimes be hard; that's why it's important to develop this clair. What does a dad feel like? What does a mom feel like? Again, it is a feeling. This is one of the strongest clairs for you to develop. That's where that gut instinct comes in—and that gut intuition is your "feeling" clair.

Information that comes through clairsentience is often very physical. I once had a Spirit who had been run over by a car. The first thing I noticed when I connected to him was a tingling in my legs. I had learned to trust those physical sensations, and just said, "What happened to his leg? Did he have a limp?"

My clairsentience has developed strongly over time, and so will yours. I have become very aware of my body, and the areas on my body that I am drawn to, during a reading. I can also detect a sudden change in energy with a Spirit. At first, they will come in excited and happy to talk to their loved one, then a major shift happens. That's when I know they may have struggled with depression or suicide—or they need to offer an apology. I have learned to interpret any shift in energy.

One of the most memorable clairsentient readings I have had was with a woman who found me on TikTok. I struggled in the beginning with her reading. She was very matter of fact and was not giving me a lot. I felt the energy that was transpiring between the two of us and could feel that the man that I was trying to bring through for her was not who she wanted. The energy was just off. I took three deep breaths, and asked Spirit to please send me the person she expected. Almost immediately, I received: female, cancer, died too young, very active. So, I felt deeper into that, and gave her the information.

She confirmed that yes, she understood all of that. The energy suddenly changed; I knew that I now had who she wanted. I went on, but I still felt the information was general, and I needed to give this lady concrete proof. I asked Spirit about her cancer: "Can you tell me what type of cancer you had? I need to give your loved one solid proof." I sat quietly and became very aware of my body. After a good fifteen seconds, I was drawn to my stomach. I turned to my client and said, "Can you tell me who the lady in Spirit is, one who died way too young from stomach cancer?" My client replied, "My daughter." From that moment on, the energy shifted completely, and everything began to flow. It was an incredible reading—filled with memories, emotions, and evidence. And all that was possible because I've learned to listen to the feelings in my body that Spirit sends me.

Clairsentient Exercises

In this exercise, you will get into a slightly relaxed state and, one at a time, you will feel the emotions, or feeling, of your mom and dad, your siblings, aunts and uncles, and grandparents. Visualize and feel your own family members. Even though people can have very different feelings about their family, what matters most for identifying relationships is what *feels* like a sister to you, what *feels* like a grandfather. When you're dealing with Spirit, because you're the conduit, you often feel the information from your point of view and from the references you have. Even if their personal relationship with their relative was very different from yours, you're learning to identify the familial relationship—the bloodline.

Sometimes I visualize the bloodline flowing; when I *feel a cut*, that tells me that the person coming through and the sitter aren't related. Then I say, "Okay, do you have a friend that maybe has passed away? Because I don't feel a blood connection." I had a reading once, where I could not get the relationship. I was struggling with it. I felt it was family, but then I felt it wasn't family. And I said, "I don't think he's family." The sitter says, "Well, he wasn't blood, but I called him uncle." Those readings are the hard ones. The Spirit seems like family because they feel so close, but when I am doing the bloodline, there isn't any. It can get confusing sometimes.

So now . . . back to the exercise. This time, feel the emotions or feelings of your best friend, your coworker, or neighbor. How might those people feel different from family? Visualize the bloodline during readings. If it is not complete, or it suddenly stops, then the person you have is probably not related.

Psychometry

Another way you can practice clairsentience is by psychometry. Find an object that belongs to somebody else and hold it. Feel and sense the energy from it. Then, write down feelings based on the object—who did the energy belong to? Was it a gift, or did the person buy it? What emotions can you tell that person had, based on the object that you're holding?

Emotion Cards

If you have an opportunity, get yourself a deck of emotion cards. Pick a card. Imagine, for example, it is the card "angry." Feel anger in your body. Where do you tighten? How does the emotion manifest in your jaw? Your belly? Your back? Then pick another card. Perhaps it might be "sad." Lean fully into the emotion. Familiarize yourself with your emotional range and responses.

My clairsentience often will express itself as an emotion, and I have learned how to recognize the meanings associated with my emotional responses. Any time I get a sad feeling, I know that I have contact with a Spirit who suffered from depression and either committed suicide or overdosed on drugs. I receive the information through the emotion of sadness. That's become my sign.

Color and Clairsentience

Picture the color orange. What does that color mean to you? For example, when I get a flash of orange, I know that the person is creative, because I have assigned that attribute to the color.

Go through the color spectrum and assign associations and meanings to colors that are unique to you. The purpose here is dual. First, this exercise offers you a chance to reflect upon, and establish associations with, different colors. Second, by doing so, you are letting Spirit know what your color associations are. In these exercises, you are building your own references. Essentially, you are creating a personal guide to the language of Spirit.

For example, let's take the color red. You can assign any meaning to it that feels right to *you*. It could be healing, or it could be anger; there is no right or wrong. This is your own key that you're creating so that you and Spirit can communicate most effectively. If I get green, I know someone needs profound healing, so I'll go into the reading focusing on the need to heal. When I use colors, Spirit doesn't have to communicate to me in a lengthy way. Instead, a color pops into my head and I know what it means, and then we'll go from there. As you build up the understanding, the meaning, of these signs or feelings—this spiritual shorthand—you can help bring so much more information through. This helps confirm for your sitter the presence of their loved one, and it can be very helpful with their healing and journey. The more information you can bring, and the more specific and accurate that information is, the better. It is often the specifics, the intimate or unique things, that make a reading powerful. Lean into that.

Blending

An advanced technique from clairsentience is called blending. In a slightly relaxed state, imagine your loved one standing right next to you. Slowly imagine your arm moving into theirs and becoming one with each other. Notice what the arms and hands of the deceased feel like—and then imagine your arms and hands blending with Spirit's arms and hands. Then merge your leg and foot with theirs. Feel what it is like to be them. This is an advanced technique, but it helps you get into the personality of the Spirit. For example, through blending, you might notice that the hands are particularly frail. Blending allows you to know the departed in a different way.

I do this sometimes just to get a man's hands. If I feel that their hands are calloused, I know that they probably did manual labor, so I can usually say, "He was a blue-collar worker," just because

I went with his hands. There's a lot you can tell from someone's hands. Using the blending technique helps connect with, and identify, Spirit.

When I first did this exercise, I chose to blend with my father. I remembered him so clearly, using a perfectly shaped circular scar that he got from burning himself while working on an engine. As I blended with him, I could feel the scar as if it were my own, and it allowed me a depth of connection that I had not felt before.

Claircognizance

Claircognizance is "clear knowing." It is just a *knowing* about something. You don't know why you know, or how you know—you just *know*. This clair helps with names, personality types, creating the story of Spirit—just about anything. It is a knowing so precise that there is no denying its accuracy.

I was in Los Angeles in 2019, taking a platform demonstration workshop. Platform demonstration is the ability to bring through Spirit in front of an audience and demonstrate mediumistic abilities. It takes unique training to learn to do this type of mediumship. I will be discussing it in more detail in a later chapter since this may be a path your mediumship takes.

I was attending with about fifteen other students, many of whom I had taken classes with previously. We had become a close-knit group. I was sitting in class this particular day, waiting for my turn to go on stage and demonstrate. I had a Spirit initiating a connection with me. The connection was so strong that I knew it was a male, and that he was here for one of my classmates, Trevor.

I also knew that this Spirit had passed from a drug overdose and had battled addiction for most of his adult life. I just knew all this information. I also knew his name was Brian—no question about it. I was very confident. That is how strong the claircognizant information was coming in.

The instructor, Colby Rebel, called my name out, and I jumped up to the front of the class. I still get very nervous speaking in front of people, and the shaking in my voice was noticeable. I began, "I have a male in Spirit who died from a drug overdose and his name was Brian. Does anyone in the class understand that?" Just as I suspected, my classmate Trevor raised his hand, with a look of shock on his face that his friend was coming through so accurately.

I even amazed myself that the information I received was so accurate. There was no interpreting anything; I wish all communication was this easy! But just like we, as humans, are all different and have different communication styles, so do those in Spirit.

Claircognizant Exercises

The "name game" is a great tool for tapping your claircognizance. Spirit can't give a name unless you have a warehouse of possible names. That's why foreign names would turn out to be so difficult for me. I didn't know many of them. Practice writing names down, as many as you can. Set a timer for two minutes. Start with the letter A, and just start writing, for two minutes. Then go on to B, and keep writing, all the way through the alphabet. Then, collect more names by looking at baby-naming websites or books, and be sure to gather names in other languages. Organize names alphabetically and then test yourself every few weeks as you build your bank of names to see how many you can recall.

A Zener Card Deck

Zener decks contain a series of cards with shapes on them; it's a favorite tool of psychics and paranormal researchers. First, you pull a card from the deck without looking at it. Feel into the card, and using your psychic abilities, sense the shape, and then see if you're right. Notice if there is a pattern in the feelings or sensations connected to your responses—both correct and incorrect ones. What kinds of feelings in your body let you know that you are spot on? What did you feel when your answers were less accurate?

Clairgustance

Clairgustance is "clear taste." For me personally, clear taste is a rare occurrence; however, for you, it may be different. You may come across a taste of something familiar in your mouth during a reading, like chocolate or any other food. Sometimes, you may even taste blood. This could be a way Spirit wants to portray their favorite food, or how they passed.

The Psychic Palette

Imagine the tastes of different foods, like chocolate. For me, the idea of tasting blood is very unappetizing, and I don't encourage it personally. However, as I mentioned earlier, you need to tune into your personal psychic palette. If you find yourself perceiving tastes during readings, or becoming very aware of them, it might turn out to be an important clair for you. If it is, just practice it like you would any other sense. Note the tastes you're getting, and any feelings or perceptions that go with them. As you start learning more, write down what those mean to you. I could see a sweet taste signifying love, or a sour taste representing a bad relationship. An off flavor could be regret. You can incorporate your sensing of flavors into your reference library for readings.

Clairalience

Clairalience is the clair of smell—and appears more frequently than taste for many mediums. For example, I had a reading where I kept smelling the sitter's grandmother. A soft, sweet fragrance surrounded me. I could sense that this was what she smelled like all the time. During the reading, I told the client, "My, your grandmother had a certain scent to her, and every time you smell that scent, it reminds you of her." And the woman said that, indeed, her grandmother had a tin full of Avon lipsticks. When she would open it, the aroma of lipsticks would drift into the air.

Another instance of clairalience might be cigarette or cigar smoke associated with the deceased. I often smell the smoke from my dad's pipe. As a matter of fact, that musty tobacco smell appeared to me four times just last week, and I knew he was around. I don't smoke, and neither does anyone else in my life. Some psychics describe smelling roses, or other flowers, from someone who has died. Clairalience is powerful evidence of Spirit's presence and reveals a lot to those of us who are doing readings.

You can heighten your ability to discern different smells when you're taking your nature walks. Pay attention as you allow yourself to breathe in the scent of the flowers, grass, trees, and everything else around you. Investigate whether you can make distinctions between similar smells—for example, the grass of a lawn and the grass near a pond.

Whenever you walk into a room, whether at a friend's house or a restaurant, breathe in, and take a moment to linger with the fragrances around you. Some places smell musty, some antiseptic, floral, or fresh. When realtors are selling houses, they often put cookies in the oven before a viewing so it smells like a home. While you're at home, notice when you're picking up any smells and identify them so you can practice your clairalience.

Synchronicities and Symbols

Spirit also speaks in synchronicities—the simultaneous occurrence of events which appear significantly related but have no discernible causal connection. Synchronicities often happen over and over again. If you are seeing numbers being repeated all around you, for example, those are synchronicities. If you habitually check the time, and the numerals repeatedly show 11:11 or some other distinctive number, that's a synchronicity. If you see those same numbers on a license plate, address, etc., the synchronicity is reinforced. Other examples would include finding the same type of coin repeatedly, seeing the same type of bird repeatedly, or having a song come up repeatedly. I tell my clients who are suffering from loss and grief to watch for synchronicities in their life because those synchronicities are their loved ones speaking to them.

Along with synchronicities, I now understand the various signs and symbols Spirit uses to communicate with me. As you develop your abilities, you will notice certain signs and symbols that Spirit uses repeatedly to deliver certain messages. Some of you may get very literal information; some of you may get symbolic information. You will receive whatever is right for you. I tend to get very literal information, and then I try to feel into the symbol for deeper meaning. Here is a sampling of the signs and symbols that I have discerned over the years:

- Saluting: someone has a connection to the military.
- Head hanging down: someone took their own life.
- Birds: the sitter sees cardinals all the time.
- Coins: the sitter finds dimes or pennies frequently.
- Clock: the sitter often sees numbers.
- Books: the Spirit or the sitter is an avid reader.
- Flowers: the Spirit liked to garden.
- Playing cards: the Spirit liked to gamble or play cards.
- Glass of whiskey: the Spirit had an alcohol problem.

Remember, Spirits use your brain, your memories, your relatability to things; they use *all of you*. They use the clairs.

Your Signs and Symbols Rotary Card File

As I mentioned above, I have come to learn that a sad feeling in my body usually indicates that someone connected to the sitter committed suicide or overdosed on drugs. That is my personal signal. In the same way, certain visual signs, smells, tastes or sounds represent other important meanings.

Every clair is a piece of the puzzle. If you want to get the whole story of a Spirit's life, you have to use all your clairs to interpret it correctly. If you just use clairvoyance, you may misinterpret what Spirit is trying to convey. For instance, picture an apple. Just using your clear-seeing, you may interpret that the Spirit liked apples. But what if I saw an apple and felt sick, and heard "cancer"? Well then, the interpretation of apple would be health. This is so different, and more accurate, than just saying Spirit liked apples. It took three clairs to get the interpretation right. If I just stuck with one clair, I wouldn't have interpreted this message correctly. A lazy medium might just say, "Oh, I just saw an apple, what does that mean for you?" A diligent medium will see the apple, feel the apple, hear the apple, sense the apple, and interpret the apple.

Create some way to organize all the things we discussed in this chapter: What do different colors, signs, emotions, symbols, songs represent to you? What are the personal associations that are unique to how you communicate with Spirit? I suggest the use of some type of rotary card file. In case you don't know, a rotary card file is a desktop card index used to catalog names, recipes, etc. on a rotating spindle, making it easy to flip through. You add cards as you build up your references. As time goes on, you'll start recognizing what things mean for you, because every medium is an individual, and we all work differently. It is not cookie cutter all the time. I like the analogy of the rotary card file because it starts

175

out blank, with nothing there yet. But as your knowledge increases from the readings you do, you'll be adding cards, building your card file, and soon, you'll have a huge list of communication tools. That's why you must build your own rotary card file: no one else can say for sure what the information that you are getting means, because the information is coming to you and through you. Spirit is tailoring it for you, and you're learning to understand it.

For example, I know that when I have a Spirit who appears to me with their head hanging down, a suicide is involved—because they come in with guilt. I know that when I am doing a reading and feel as though I want to lower my head, Spirit is taking responsibility for passing. I also get Spirits who look calm and inspire me to salute. That's my sign that they were in the military. Sometimes, I'll get an image of a waving flag to signify that the deceased was in the service.

You will get to know your signs and develop your own dictionary of the ways that Spirit communicates to you and what those signs mean. The only way to do that is through practice, and then documenting it using your journaling. When you get something, even if you get it wrong, go back and journal it, and guess what it really meant. In your development, you're going to start building your own rotary card file, and that will be your go-to for Spirit. Learn what all the images, sounds, smells, tastes, and feelings mean to you, and then you will have begun to master the clairs.

Using all the clairs is how you put the puzzle of the Spirit together. Remember, Spirit is using your mind, and you are hearing, seeing, feeling, smelling, and sensing its communications. The analytical left brain tends to jump to conclusions, but you need to dig deeper, using all your senses to put together the pieces, and getting a full portrait of the deceased. You need to understand what every sign and symbol means, why Spirit gave each of them to you, and decipher how each one of them is significant to the life of the Spirit, and to the sitter. This requires you to maintain intense focus and give a full effort to your reading. Sitting in your power and being healthy are important because mediumship makes big demands of you, and you want to be able to stand up to the challenge.

Being a psychic medium is something you can learn, practice, and improve upon. When you put in the time, work to hone your skills, and build your rotary card file of signs and symbols, giving your all, you can bring through truly amazing information. You can create something enchanting. You can heal a sitter's pain, like Jennifer Farmer did for me. That's what I strive for with every reading I do. I never know when the information I give will be the thing that frees someone from suffering and gives them the closure they need to move forward. For this reason, I am always writing down the meanings of the information I receive, and I make an effort to show up at my best for every reading. I am here to create healing and do something magical for people. And I believe you are being called as well.

CHAPTER EIGHT

YOUR DEVELOPMENT JOURNEY

Work from your heart space, not your head space.
-Colby Rebel

The journey of becoming a medium is powerful and exciting. For all the times you'll feel overwhelmed and wracked with doubt, you'll also have times of certainty, truth, and beautiful moments. Your psychic development will take you through your fear to a place of strength. The journey asks a lot of you, so it is very important from the start that you set your intentions, and state for yourself what you are aiming to do and why.

Write down what your intentions are and say them aloud so that the Universe can open the right doors for you. In the beginning, I sought out validation from others to make sure that this was the path for me. I finally learned that this is the path that *I* have chosen—and it has always been up to me. If I wanted it, I could have it. I just had to set my intention, and then demonstrate my commitment to the Universe by taking action.

Finding Your Why

The first key is to fully understand your *why*: Why do you want to do this work? Determine the most compelling reason you can, something with great meaning to you, and turn it into your mission statement. Make it your "Yes, I will!" to prepare for those days when everything seems to scream "No, you won't!"

Your mission statement will help you keep the course throughout your entire journey. Mediumship is not for most people: it is hard, and it involves putting aside one's ego—and investing in one's heart and soul. It can be terrifying to open up to criticism and to people's pain and suffering. You will need a powerful reason to keep going when things are hard, when you get things wrong, and when you most want to quit. Your *why* will get you through only if it is significant enough to you.

My *why* was my dad's passing. My grief over his unexpected death inspired my interest in the Spirit world and my desire to connect with him. My experience with Jennifer Farmer was so deeply healing that I never sought a medium again. I experienced real closure during that reading; it was exactly what I needed to hear, and it helped start my healing journey. And that became my why—I wanted to help others heal as I did and show them the magic that waits for us in Spirit.

It saddens me that not everybody experiences it, since they often cannot see what exists beyond their grief and loss. My intention is to help others to create the spiritual connections that will lessen the fear and pain. All of these things became my *why*.

Think carefully about what makes you want to do this work. Nail down a moment or a feeling, something strongly meaningful to you. Maybe it is a person that you wish you could have helped, or a loved one that suffered after the death of someone dear to them. Perhaps it is someone to whom you wanted to give the gift of connection and offer proof of the afterlife.

Maybe it is how you felt the first time you communicated with someone who had passed on, and you want to share that elation or that peace. Whatever you decide on as your *why*, write it down in the most simple and compelling way. It could be something like, "I will help people realize that their loved ones are still with them as I experienced with my grandmother," or "I want to spread the peace I felt when I received a message from my mother, after her passing, with as many people as I can."

You can always change your statement later if you find something more meaningful, because it is yours, after all. You just want something you can read, or repeat to yourself fairly easily, whenever you feel challenged—and you will probably feel challenged a lot over the course of your development! You may want to write your mission on a card and keep it in your purse or wallet. Once you know your *why*, your challenges take on a different meaning. They aren't there as proof you shouldn't be doing this; they are there to be overcome. If you can give healing to even one person who desperately needs it, or bring love or faith to someone, you will have done something transformative. Your *why* will always remind you of your reason for showing up. Find your *why*.

Building Your Foundation

Once you have set your intention and understood your *why*, and created your mission statement, it is time to build your foundation.

There are six steps to building your foundation and your development:

Step One: Meditate and sit in the power at least three to four times a week.

Step Two: Heal your traumas and raise your vibration through gratitude, affirmations, manifesting statements, and journaling.

Step Three: Sit with your guides at least a couple of times a week.

Step Four: Do exercises to strengthen your psychic ability. Remember, every medium is a psychic, but not every psychic is a medium. In order to be a medium, you must develop both.

Step Five: Practice with friends and family. Join psychic development circles online or at local venues. Take classes and workshops. Start building your personal Spirit rotary card file of signs, symbols, and meanings.

Step Six: Do it! Start reading for people. Join psychic fairs and online groups to practice your skills.

Let's expound on each step in detail.

Step One: Meditate

Meditation calms your mind, silences your left brain, and creates space to connect to Spirit. As you recall, sitting in power is about building inner and external power so that you can sustain energy.

It's not about connecting to anybody; it's about building your own energetic field. This is like working a muscle—the more you work it, the more you exercise it, the stronger it becomes. The more psychic fitness you have, the easier it will be to sustain your focus and vitality for most accurate readings.

Step Two: Do Your Inner Work

Do your inner work. This involves personal healing and raising your vibration so that you have more to offer. By doing so, you bring more joy and gratitude into your life, and you set yourself up to connect clearly with Spirit (with less of your own pain or unhappiness to get in the way). It frees you up to bring more of who you are to your clients. Focusing on your inner process results in you bringing more love and healing to your readings, which you can only do if you've given yourself that gift first.

Step Three: Sit with Your Guides

Your guides are there to help you through the process. In time, they will let you know what their specific roles are and how you can call upon them. Connect to your guides a few times a week, and your communication will deepen.

Step Four: Do Psychic Exercises

Develop your clairs through the activities I discussed in the last chapter. Choose a clair and work on it throughout the whole day; continue exercising those muscles and doing your psychic sit-ups. Work on strengthening every single clair because, remember, it's like a puzzle—you need them all. You can't just depend on your strongest clair; you must develop each one to its fullest potential. Aim to do these exercises at least three times a week.

Step Five: Practice, Practice, Practice

Get comfortable contacting Spirit in front of someone else. Practice as much as you can. Start by offering readings to friends and family, and then find groups online. Hone your abilities and gain confidence by actually doing readings for people. Work on your introduction (which we will be discussing in the next chapter), your presence and presentation, your wording, and the message you leave with your clients. Classes and workshops are great for this as well.

Step Six: Do It!

Last, you have to jump in and do it! Offer readings at psychic fairs, on Facebook, TikTok, or your own website; whatever way you want to go about it, get out there! This last step can be the scariest, but you have to take it. It may be the hardest one, but it's where you're going to learn the most.

Getting Nos and Finding Yeses

You're not going to get things right every time. There will be readings when Spirit is going to communicate with you in a manner you don't understand, or you are going to get in the way by misinterpreting something. At times, you may have the right information, and clients won't understand it because they forgot or overlooked something. There can be communication problems in every direction—I can almost guarantee it.

You do not need to be afraid of a client responding to your inquiries or statements with a "no." A no is an opportunity to go back and figure out where you went wrong and work through it. You have to get some nos so that you can learn what it feels like to be out of sync with Spirit, and to recognize when your brain is filling in the blanks. Remember, you work for Spirit.

Part of what you have to learn as a medium is to keep your cool and keep going. Be honest. If you're struggling with a connection, or the Spirit that the sitter wants is not coming through, allow the sitter to be part of the process. Hopefully, if you keep focusing in on the questions you are asking and are open to what you receive, you'll end up with the information that's needed. Each reading will be different; that's what makes mediumship a little difficult. You can be the very best, but you can have an off-Spirit or off-day. Just do your best, and with the best of intentions. If you don't have a strong connection, just say so. Be honest.

I can remember a specific reading in which I was completely off on the evidence of my client's late husband. During that reading, I had to admit to her, "I am struggling with this connection." I had contacted her husband, and he was showing me his hands. As this was usually a sign of hard labor, I said, "He was such a hard blue-collar worker." She said he wasn't.

"Okay, then," I said honestly, "Let me try that again. He keeps showing me his hands."

"No. That's totally off," she shook her head again. "He was not a hard worker, a laborer, at all. He was a banker . . . ."

As I have struggled with some connections, so will you. It's going to happen. Remember, it's not about me or you. Spirit has to be able to communicate effectively with me as much as I have to interpret the meaning. Mediumship is a three-way communication process: Spirit communicates with me; I have to interpret so the client understands; and the client has to receive the message and remember the information. If I have Spirits who are not communicating the way I need, I can't take that personally. I have to put my ego aside and admit that I may not be the medium for them.

Remember the banker I mentioned above? Well, it turns out he was a gardener; he loved to garden, and that was why he was showing me his dirty hands. Spirit is never wrong. It was my interpretation that was wrong. What I learned from that experience is that, in the future, when I "see" dirty hands, I need to go deeper and ask, "Why are they dirty?" For me, this was among the great lessons that only come with practice.

We are all human and are going to make mistakes, and sometimes we will interpret symbols and signs incorrectly. Just remember, every "no" is an opportunity for you to lean into the feeling again and ask Spirit to elaborate: "Why are your hands the way they are? What are you doing with your hands?" That's how you turn a "no" into a "yes."

I explain at the beginning of each reading, "I don't see Spirit. I don't hear them, either. Everything that happens is happening in my brain and in all my senses, in my body. I may interpret something incorrectly, but if we work together, the message will come through."

And so that's what we do: We work it out.

When Too Much Detail is Too Much

There are times to avoid giving too much detail. When I am in a mediumship reading, I stay away from physical descriptions. Remember: we don't see the departed in physical form. We get a feeling, and an idea, or maybe even a flash of a picture, in our brain. Our left brain will fill in the blanks and create something. Sometimes Spirit will use our own memory bank of people and relatives. Be very careful getting caught up in the details of what you "see" and using specific descriptions.

For example, if I say, "I am connecting with a grandmother in Spirit who died of cancer and loved to cook," I will most likely get a "yes" (assuming that is what Spirit showed me). But if I say, "She was the cutest little old lady with pitch black hair, who is wearing a dark-colored dress with red shoes, has her hair pinned back and is wearing bright lipstick," I may get a "no" because her grandmother was a brunette who never wore lipstick. Now I've lost our rapport. However, Spirit might be sending me the meaning "grandmother" through *my* visual idea of a grandmother, which is the one I de-scribed with black hair and make-up.

Try to avoid digging yourself into a hole. If you are going to use descriptions, break up the description into bite-size pieces of info. It is easier to narrow down what you got wrong and go back in and feel into it again. If you list ten specific things before you check in with your sitter, it can be hard to dig yourself out of that. I suggest listing two or three pieces of information first, then check in with the sitter to see if you are on the right track. Be cautious, however, that you are not spending the whole reading simply describing in detail what you are visualizing.

Remember the woman whose husband was a gardener? She was so focused on wanting to hear from him that I could have had her grandfather or somebody else in her family, but she kept saying "no" to all the evidence I was providing. She wanted so badly to hear from her husband that she wasn't open to any other possibilities.

However, the minute I took a deep breath and just surrendered, a flash of a cardinal came to mind. I sensed there was a deeper meaning to the symbol. "There's more," I told her. "I know there's more." She asked what I meant. I didn't know, I just felt as though there was something else to do with the bird.

"Did he have birds?" I asked.

"No."

"Did you have bird feeders in the yard?"

"No."

I still didn't know what it could have been, but he continued to tell me that it is more than just the bird. This is where I had no knowledge in my own memory bank for Spirit to use. I just knew that the cardinal meant something to him specifically. I discovered at the end of the reading that he was a big Arizona Cardinals football fan! Another great lesson. I needed to learn more about football!

That particular day, I can remember just being off in every reading I did. I couldn't figure out what was going on. In every reading I had, I kept getting a male in his fifties who passed away. I was doing a series of short readings, and I was just getting things wrong. I always write down the piece of evidence that I get a "no" for.

"I have a man who liked to play pool?"

"Nope, no pool," said one sitter.

"I have a man who talks about football."

"No, no football," said another sitter.

As it turned out, the husband who loved the Arizona Cardinals was coming through the whole time. He was showing up in every reading! When I finally realized this, toward the end of my reading with his wife, I said, "Hold on . . . did he love pool?" Yes, he did! All the nos from the previous readings finally came up as yeses.

I then looked at the clock and realized that I had been running late for her appointment. He showed up for his reading on time, but I was still reading for other people. It was as if he had the attitude, "You're on my time, and I am here because it is my time." Needless to say, he was probably very punctual during his days on Earth!

During another reading, out of nowhere, I thought of horses. Spirit didn't say, "Oh, I used to train your mother to ride horses." Simply, the thought of horses imprinted itself in my mind, and I had to figure out what the image meant.

"Your grandfather just showed me horses," I told the sitter, "and I feel like maybe you would have been raised around horses."

The sitter said, "No."

I had to then go back in and ask her grandfather about the horses and what the connection was. I then had an awareness of the word mother. I asked the sitter if her mother had a connection to horses. She replied, "Yes."

This example is why learning and developing the clairs is so important. If we were all able to hear Spirit in full sentences, we wouldn't need anything·else because it would just be so easy to understand Spirit. Unfortunately, that is not how it works most of the time. There can be exceptions, for sure, but in most cases, in a professional reading, mediums interpret the information they are receiving. It is a flash, a thought, a feeling.

Let me give you another example of how I sometimes use multiple clairs to interpret information correctly. I had a great reading with a woman who wanted to connect with her mother. Her mom came through and spoke of cancer, and then I got a thought around a picture. Specifically, I got the word "picture." I had a knowing that there was something about this picture, so I used my clairsentience, and I just felt into it. I suddenly had a knowing that people were arguing over a picture and wanted to make sure it was the right picture, and that mom would have liked the picture that they chose. I didn't hear the words. It was just claircognizance.

I trusted my knowing and said, "Your mom is talking about a picture, and that you all are fighting over what picture to use, and you didn't think that she would like the picture that you chose."

The woman started crying deeply, "We were just trying to pick what picture would go on her headstone. And everyone was fighting because the one that got picked was one that they didn't think that she would like."

I find it miraculous that the information comes through, but that's what comes with experience. You will learn, in time, to just trust what you get, to go for it, and to not be afraid.

As soon as you get a no, you will often feel like shutting down. You have to keep going and work through it. During a reading, I make a "no" column on a piece of paper, where I write down all the nos, and I say, "We'll go back to the nos at the end."

Eventually, we'll figure it out and, nine times out of ten, it is just that the sitter didn't remember something the first time around. During one reading, I had a lady whose husband in Spirit was showing me the number nine. The nine, the nine . . . was September important to her, or anything about the number nine? She said "no" to everything.

I said, "Okay, well, I'm just going to write it down, and we can revisit it at the end of the reading."

Later in the session, she said, "Oh, my God! The ninth is our anniversary!" She had forgotten, but he remembered!

Psychic Amnesia

There is a term—psychic amnesia—that can affect sitters. The sitter also often feels under pressure when they're sitting in front of a medium. Sometimes they won't remember important things until later. I let my sitter know that I am keeping track of the things that we have not been able to validate. I say, "Here's my 'no' column. If I get a no, this is where I am going to put it." Most of the time, by the end of the reading, the nos become yeses as the sitter remembers certain details. Sometimes it might be a few days or weeks, but the person will contact me and say, "Oh, my God! You were right!"

Fear and Discomfort

During your journey, you're going to have to get comfortable being uncomfortable. You're going to be scared to death when you're doing your very first reading. You're probably going to meditate for three hours before you do that reading just because you want to get all the information that you can before you meet the sitter. You're going to be afraid to reveal something that you get from Spirit because you're terrified it's going to be wrong.

These are all the feelings that I had throughout my whole journey. I was still petrified before a reading as recently as a year ago, before I sat down to write this book. In the beginning, I had a fear before every reading that it wasn't going to go well. And every reading was just fine. A big part of what helped me through that fear was doing psychic fairs—getting out there, doing a lot of readings. I just had to jump in and put myself in situations where I couldn't overthink things. So, practice, and then practice some more. Practice on people who don't care if you get it wrong, just so you can practice, because that's how you build your confidence.

Psychic fairs are a great opportunity. One valuable aspect of them is that they help your endurance, because they can be as long as six hours. When you're working for six hours straight, and you're speed-reading people every twenty minutes, you're abruptly switching to another energy, another Spirit. Going from one reading right into the next one will help you sustain long periods of energy. Because you're doing consecutive readings, one right after another, you're thinking about just getting through every twenty minutes, and then resetting yourself for the next one. You hope and pray that you're right, and that you're good, and you just have to push through it.

In addition to the fairs, take as many classes as you can. See if you can find a local circle. If not, try and build one with some of your friends and get together every week to practice bringing in Spirit.

Although I had been intensely practicing and doing classes since 2016, it wasn't until March of 2021 that I finally gained confidence in it. Why? I began using the social media platform TikTok to find clients, and I expanded my business exponentially. I grew to about 23,000 followers there, and I became inundated with readings. I suddenly had no time to be nervous and afraid anymore. I had to push forward and get through the seven or eight readings that I had booked every night. There was no time for meditation, and no time for fear or insecurities. I had to get comfortable being uncomfortable—and just do it!

I am past that fear now, for the most part. Based on experience, every reading offers something positive to the sitter. Some are better than others, but they are all good, and healing. It took me doing over six hundred readings in the span of eight months to gain the confidence that I have because I didn't fail anyone; I've never flat-out failed. Yes, I got a few things wrong, and that's okay—I am still a human fighting with my own brain sometimes. However, it has always turned out that what I got right was so powerful that the sitter forgot anything that I got wrong. Little misses don't matter to the sitter if you offer something that resonates deeply, and the person walks away knowing contact was verifiably made with the other side. That, in itself, is so powerful.

Take my prior example of the cardinal. My sitter didn't care if I got it wrong that her husband was a blue-collar worker. I got the cardinal, and even that I didn't get exactly right. But once she knew where I was going, and knew what I was talking about, she was the sweetest lady. She even messaged me afterwards to ask me to mentor her to be able to connect with Spirit. So even if I thought that it wasn't the best reading, she got what she needed out of it. That's the magic of mediumship.

Certifications/Mentorships

Although certifications are not necessary for becoming a professional medium, I do find that it gives one a level of credibility. Spirit led me to learn of Lisa Williams and a certification course she had available. It was a twelve-week course that involved inner work, psychic work, and mediumship work. Enrollees had to select a master trainer who would work closely with them. I had learned of the course by watching a psychic medium on Facebook, Colby Rebel. I was immediately drawn to this lady from Jersey who had a strong, no-nonsense personality. I watched her for months every day when she went live on Facebook. Little did I know then what impact she would have on me and my future as a medium.

I spent twelve long weeks studying and doing all the exercises and healing work under Lisa's program. At the end of the three months, I had to fly to work with my master teacher to do an in-person workshop and final testing. I spent all of Friday and Saturday in a workshop practicing, practicing, and more practicing under the guidance of Colby. Then, on Sunday, I was tested to become certified.

We were expected to come to the Colby Rebel Spiritual Center in Los Angeles dressed professionally and prepared to give readings that would be our final exam. The first item was the psychic test. It was a blind reading. We knew nothing about the person, not even the first name. We all waited outside, and Colby brought the volunteers in. One by one, we lined up and went and sat in front of each volunteer. On the wall in front of us all was a timer that was set for forty-five minutes. Our assignment was to complete readings for three separate volunteers in a row, with each reading being forty-five minutes long.

Each reading had to include each person's relationships, career, finances, health, and any legal issues they may have. The volunteers were instructed to give zero feedback. They couldn't say "yes", they couldn't say "no"; they were to just sit there for forty-five minutes with arms crossed and no facial expression. After the reading, the volunteer would complete a form to provide feedback on the accuracy of the reading. You had to have done well on each reading in order to be a certified psychic under Lisa Williams's Independent School of Spiritual Development. Just when we thought we were done, we had to line up to do it all over again for the mediumship testing.

Those certifications were probably the most terrifying things I've ever put myself through. Yes—I wanted to run, wanted to hide. I wanted to say, "Screw this! Why am I doing this to myself? Like, why? Why? Why am I putting myself through all this torture?" (You see how important it is to remember your WHY!)

But I pushed through; I did it. I sat down and gave it my all each time, for each of the volunteers. Then I waited. It was probably a week or two later that I got the call telling me I'd passed, that I was certified.

The sense of accomplishment was so strong. I needed to do it. Any time we put ourselves out there and do something we don't think we can, our confidence increases. You also will discover that you are capable of more than you know. Your world and the possibilities you see for yourself get a little bit bigger. Always push yourself, and if you feel called to try something that seems beyond you, remember that you are always growing, and that what was once out of reach may soon be within your grasp.

It is natural for you to want to seek out a mentor—someone who has experienced being new to this world and who has succeeded in developing their gifts to a professional level. After completing the Lisa Williams training, I knew that Colby Rebel would be that person for me. I wanted to learn everything I could from her. She was a tough teacher. She did not let me get in the way of myself. She pushed me to places I never thought I could go. She was exactly what I needed to keep me accountable to this journey.

I took every class I could with her. I paid for private mentorship opportunities when they were available. Was it easy? Absolutely not. I cried many tears of frustration, felt disappointed with myself, thought I let her down when I did not do well, always wanting to make her proud. Eventually, all those hours of work, the money spent, and the time away from home paid off. My investment in myself with a teacher who would push me past all my comfort zones gave me the confidence I needed to go professional. I owe a lot to, and am forever grateful to, Colby Rebel. She saw in me what I couldn't recognize in myself. I encourage you to find someone who will inspire you and mentor you into your most professional, confident self.

A Road Map

Everyone's development will be different. I will give you a road map, but know that you can take detours. You are finding the path that works best for you. The timing will be different for everyone. Some will move through the steps quickly; others will take more time. Move through the steps at *your* comfort level. You may have to go back and revisit the healing process because something will trigger you. You will never "finish" learning all that you can. You will continue to strengthen your clairs for years to come. The steps are fluid and are an important part of your mediumship practice.

Earlier, I mentioned the components necessary for successful psychic development. I am going to review them here and offer some timelines.

1. Meditate/Sit in the Power: Dedicate one to two months to mastering the art of meditation and sitting in the power. This will become a permanent part of your mediumship discipline.

2. Heal Your Traumas and Raise Your Vibration: Dedicate as much time as you need to heal through gratitude, affirmations, and journaling. You may revisit this step often as things come up in your life. The key is raising your vibration and becoming happy from the inside out.

3. Know Your Guides: You may choose to work with your guides or not. Spend as much time as you need developing those relationships, and then do what resonates with you. They can bring you support and guidance but are not necessary for successful mediumship.

4. Develop all Your Clairs: Developing the clairs, however, is critical to your growth as a medium. Doing so will require most of your time and focus. Practice with the exercises in Chapter Seven. Do readings for family and friends. Join development circles. Take classes. There is no timeline; don't compare your journey to someone else's. Divine timing is everything—and necessary to cultivate skill, trust, surrender, and confidence.

5. Become a Professional Medium: When you are ready, just do it! You may never feel as if you are ready—you just have to commit to it at some point. I would recommend starting by offering free readings to people, just to practice. When there is no money attached, you don't feel the desperate need to be right; it takes some of the pressure off. Commit to a hundred practice readings.

Social media can greatly increase your opportunities. Create pages on Facebook, Instagram, and TikTok. Start by offering affordable readings to build your reviews and referrals. You can then increase your rates as you become recognized, which will take time and patience. I was doing five to ten readings a week for two years before my business took off.

As you gain more skill and mastery, you will need to trust your connection. This is where self-work is very important. Remember, whatever is wrong in your mediumship is what's wrong in your own life. It is essential to your mediumship development, especially in the beginning, to work on healing your triggers and raising your vibration simultaneously.

No one wakes up one day and becomes a professional medium. Generally, it takes about five years to fully develop one's craft and establish one's reputation.

The journey is a long one, and it can be overwhelming as there are so many aspects to it: your personal healing and confidence, meditation skills, connection to Spirit, mastery of the clairs, presentation, and relationships with clients. However, when it all comes together, you will discover that your life has changed.

I have been transformed by my journey so far. I am stronger, happier, and more fully alive than I've ever been. This is the path that I was meant to walk, and if it is meant for you, you'll find that it is the best thing you can do. Embrace the journey and enjoy as much as you can along the way. Follow your path and . . . get walking!

CHAPTER NINE

STRUCTURE OF A READING

Let your intuition guide you, but also use your head and take responsibility for the free will choices you make.
-Theresa Caputo

In this chapter, I will teach you how to structure a reading. By now, you have been journaling, meditating, sitting in the power, getting in touch with Spirit, and developing all your clairs. When you start giving readings, whether to friends and family, online development groups, or in class settings, you'll want to have a consistent format that will enable you to focus on Spirit and the task at hand. This helps guide you through the reading and ensures that the sitter gets the best possible experience. The structure of your readings will alter and improve over time as you find what works best for you.

The format is, by no means, set in stone. It is merely a guide for you to use while you develop. Creating your own style is more important, and that will come with time. You want to find a way of presenting that puts your client at ease, is authentic for you, and helps facilitate communication between Spirit, the sitter, and you.

You will first craft your opening, creating an introduction that draws the sitter in and gives them safety and reassurance. This may sound simple, but when my former tutor, John Johnson, asked me what my opening was, I didn't know what to say. He explained to me that the opening tells the sitter what to expect from the reading and makes the person feel more comfortable. You'll use your opening to describe how you work, because not all reading styles are alike. Think about your opening and write it down in your journal. I will give you mine as an example:

Hi, thank you for booking with me. Have you ever had a reading before? Well, Spiritual readers all work a little bit differently, so let me explain how I work so you will know what to expect during our session today. I am a psychic medium, which means I work both psychically and mediumistically. On a psychic level, my soul and guides connect to your soul and guides to deliver information to you regarding career, health, relationships, finances, and legal issues. On a mediumistic level, I feel Spirit first. I distinguish male from female Spirits by noticing on which side of my body I feel sensations. Once I establish the connection, Spirit uses my mind, memories, body, and all my senses to communicate. It is my job to interpret what they are saying and deliver it to you in such a way that you will understand. I will just need a "yes," "no," or "I don't know" from you. Sound good?

That is the opening I use for every reading I do. It lets my sitter know exactly what to expect from me, and what their job as the sitter is. Once you have gone over your opening with the sitter, sit in stillness, take three deep breaths, and make a connection to a Spirit in the Spirit world. This will be different for everyone. I know when I am connecting because I start to get tingles on my head. Others may feel, sense, or know if you have a male or female. Some of you will just have a sense, or a knowing. For me, my right side represents male, and my left represents female. Lock in the connection once you have the gender.

Next, you want to sense, feel, or know how they passed, who they are, what they did for a living, etc. You will start out feeling as if you are making things up because Spirit uses your thoughts, memories, and senses to communicate. Eventually you will learn to "feel" the difference in what your own thoughts are and what comes from Spirit. This takes time and practice; things will all start to unfold.

Determine who you have present in Spirit. We do this by giving a few hard facts about the Spirit. Hard facts can be things such as gender, relationship, cause of death, occupation, number of children, where he/she lived, any physical ailments they may have had, etc. A hard fact is just that—a fact. It is not based on perception. These are the things you will use to determine who the Spirit is. The Spirit's relationship to the sitter can be tricky to ascertain. Sometimes you will just know, but some relationships can be difficult to understand. That's okay. If you don't have a secure answer on the relationship, use other hard facts to determine who the Spirit is.

Be very careful using physical descriptions. It's easy for our left brain to stereotype those who come to us from the Spirit world. We can assume details about their character and life based on what we see in our mind's eye. However, sometimes what we see in our mind's eye is not the true story. As I discussed in an earlier chapter, if you get into too much detail, you can find yourself backed into a corner.

Spirit uses an image to convey a piece of evidence. The evidence is not always meant to include every inch of detail. Take my example of a Spirit giving me an image of a grandmother, to get me to say "grandmother." If I zoomed in and began to describe how this grandmother looks, what she wore, the color of her dress, the type of shoes, etc., then I have a great chance of being wrong because that was not the intent of the image. I was merely supposed to say "grandmother."

You will undoubtedly fall into this trap in the early stages of your development. You are going to be so excited that you got an image, that you're going to want to explain every detail of it. You will learn rather quickly that you can't always rely on the details of an image. You may get lucky at first and get it right, but the Spirits are our teachers, and they will show you in another instance that the details do not matter.

Cause of death is an exceptionally good piece of evidence, a good example of the hard facts you seek. But don't force it; sometimes you will know exactly how someone passed, no question! Sometimes you will have a Spirit who won't even talk about it. If you are just trying to go down a checklist of items, looking for hard facts, you are not being authentic to Spirit. Let them guide the conversation.

Practice One: Coming Up with the Hard Facts

Practice on a friend or family member. Take three deep, cleansing breaths and make a connection. Come up with three or four hard facts about the contact you have made. Practice this two to three times, making communication with a different Spirit each time.

You can repeat this as many times, and with as many people, as you want. This exercise will help you establish a connection with Spirit, determine their relationship to the sitter, and learn their cause of death, occupations, etc.

Once you have established who you have—e.g., "I have a male who is in Spirit, who died from heart failure, was a blue-collar worker, feels like a grandfather"—you can then build off the energy, and begin to get to know him. This is where soft facts come into the reading. Soft facts are things such as the Spirit's personality, likes and dislikes, hobbies, and memories. For example, a grandfather may tell me that he loved the outdoors, and fishing was his favorite pastime. As the sitter, you would remember that time he took you fishing and you caught this big trout (well, he caught it, and made you think you did). You were so proud of yourself and couldn't wait to run home and tell your mom. Your grandfather was a kind man who never met a stranger; he used to talk to everyone. He tells me your grandmother would get so annoyed because they could never go anywhere without him talking with strangers and taking up an hour's time. He even tells me that there was this one time she got so angry with him for doing so that she walked home and just left him there.

You can build off soft facts multiple times and give multiple memories, depending on timing of the reading. Spirit is very intelligent and will give you important facts at the beginning of the reading that you can always elaborate on. This is what we call *layering the evidence*: getting a few pieces of information about a Spirit, and then building off of each one. In the above example, I could have just ended the evidence about his hobby with just fishing. Instead, I took fishing and layered into it. I had a conversation with Grandpa and asked, "Well, what is your favorite memory of fishing? Was it a small fish or a big fish? What happened next?"

See? It is a two-way conversation. Using this technique eliminates the "drip" that most early developing mediums struggle with. The drip is when you, the medium, are just waiting for information to drop in. It is comparable to a dripping faucet. You don't want a dripping faucet; you want a flowing faucet—and to do that, you must engage in conversation.

Another example would be if I have a mother in Spirit who died of cancer. She became quite sick during that experience and wants to thank everyone who came to help her. She was a very prideful individual and hated that she needed help. She tells me that the sitter has a picture of her, someone is getting a tattoo, and she brings up your father. With the information I just gave, I can now go back and ask mom, "What about the picture? Why is that important to your daughter? Where is the picture? Do you like the picture? Who is getting the tattoo? What is the tattoo of? Does someone already have a tattoo? Did you like tattoos? What about Dad? Is he doing okay? Why are you bringing up Dad?"

By asking questions and getting curious, you can build the reading without waiting for things to "drop in." Remember, this is someone's loved one. Bring the Spirit to life. Get to know the Spirit's personality. Add some depth to your reading.

Another strategy I have used is called the "bubble technique." Make your connections, and then get six things that come to you right away and circle them. From those six things, select one and branch-off three things about it. Select another main circled item, and branch-off three things you get about that evidence. Now you have two major pieces of evidence, and six supporting pieces of evidence, from which to build your reading. Then you can begin to unfold each one to create the story. Remember, Rome wasn't built in a day, and neither will your mediumship be. Go for it. Say what you get and don't hold back. The "wow factor" evidence comes when you say things that you think have no way of being correct. In that case, trust what Spirit gives you and speak it. This takes execution—and a lot of practice.

Practice Two: The Bubble Technique

Find someone to practice with. Take three cleansing breaths and establish a connection with someone in the Spirit world. On a piece of paper, write down six pieces of evidence that come to you. Circle each item. Go back and choose three that you want to dive into deeper. From each one you selected, come up with three more bubbles or things about the main topic. Now talk about those with your sitter and unfold the story of their loved one.

During your readings, it is always possible that you will have multiple Spirits coming through at once. You are double- (and sometimes triple-) linking. Having multiple Spirits come through in a reading has definitely happened to me. Sometimes if I have back-to-back readings, I will have information coming in during one reading that isn't making sense, such as in the case I described in the last chapter where the Spirit was "on time" for the reading.

It doesn't happen a lot, but it does happen. I just explain to the client who cannot take the information I am giving, that I may have another Spirit connecting with me who belongs to a client I am seeing later. In every reading, I keep a notebook. For each connection I make, I will write down the relationship to the sitter. As things come through, I will make a notation under the person it belongs to. It can get really tricky, but this will become easier once you have more experience. Spirit will continue to push you beyond what you ever thought was possible.

The last part of any reading is the message. Why did the Spirit come through? What does Spirit have to tell the sitter? Throughout the entire reading, you are providing evidence of the Spirit to the sitter—proving life after death—and showing the sitter that you have their loved one present with you.

The healing begins with the message. Spirit is there to give the sitter closure, offer an apology, provide support or comfort, share words of love. The message should be comforting and healing and be relevant to what the sitter needs to hear. Messages can either be easy for people or difficult. If you are blocking your emotions, messages will be more difficult for you to discern. Allow yourself to be more vulnerable and feel the emotions that you are receiving from Spirit. This is Spirits' chance to once again let the people they love know that their loved one in Spirit is okay, and that they are always available. Touch the sitter's soul and provide healing.

Some examples of messages:

I am always with you through the good times and the rough ones.

You have nothing to feel guilty about.

I am so sorry for the hurt I caused you.

You are never alone.

I believe in you.

I come to you in your dreams to support you.

I am in a place of pure, unconditional love.

I am very proud of you.

I am no longer in pain.

I am always just a thought away.

I am by your side—guiding you and helping you.

If only I had known then what I know now, I would have done things differently.

I am sorry; please forgive me.

Messages from the Spirit world are always loving and kind. Mediums who have not healed completely can put a negative spin on a reading. We allow our own life filters to interfere and skew the information we are receiving. If you have a healed and pure heart, like Spirit, the message will always be one of love.

- The structure of a reading, to recap:
- Deliver your opening.
- Make a connection/establish a link with Spirit.
- Share three or four hard facts about Spirit.
- Offer two or three soft facts about Spirit.
- Give the message from Spirit.

Practice Three: Delivering a Healing Message

Using a deck of angel cards, practice delivering messages. Pull a card and use the message and the artwork on the card to create a loving and healing message for your sitter. You can practice this on friends and family.

All of this is only a framework for you. You will find what works best for you over time. This is, again, where practice comes in. If you've only done this a few times, you're going to be very uncertain and won't even necessarily know what's working. If you've done this a few hundred times, it will become second nature. You'll know what to say and when to say it, and how to read the body language, to see if the sitter needs some time or reassurance. You'll know when to slow down, when to go deeper. It all starts to flow.

Practice on everyone you can and start creating your own style. Keep a journal and write down after each reading (or at the end of the day if you are doing a series of readings, one after another): what you did, what worked, what you want to change. Keep refining your method. Make sure you are being authentic to yourself. If you're outgoing, let yourself engage and talk a little more—be friendly. If you tend to be more reserved, be true to that. Don't fake it and try to put on a show. Find the version that feels right for you and creates the best possible experience for your sitter. Don't worry about messing up. Having a structure helps keep you on track and gives you something to follow so you don't get lost along the way.

As long as you give your sitters a positive experience, and as long as they come away knowing they connected with their loved one and got a healing message to take with them, they'll get what they needed from the reading. Your structure helps make sure that happens, and that you and your sitter get there as partners in the experience. Use the structure and make it your own, and eventually you'll be able to provide people with something truly miraculous, each and every time.

CHAPTER TEN

ETHICS

Some people can touch your life for a brief moment but will leave
an imprint for a lifetime.
-Lisa Williams

Becoming an accomplished medium will be one of your biggest challenges in life and is an amazing gift that you can give to others, but it comes with a great deal of responsibility as well. People who seek you out will be opening up to a stranger about their most significant pains, griefs, and losses. Although you are not a counselor, you will be a witness to their intimate thoughts, feelings, and relationships. They will be trusting you with details of their private lives and pain. You must treat the relationship between you and your sitter as sacred. For these reasons, it is very important to follow a code of ethics. It is crucial for you to honor their privacy, protect them from even unintentional harm, and maintain your integrity. I am going to give you some advice based on what I've learned over time, and hopefully spare you some of the difficulties that I've experienced.

As a professional psychic medium, you will have people from all walks of life come to you for readings. Not all readings will be pleasant. You will be faced with sexual and domestic abuse survivors, substance abuse, mental illness, loss of children, suicide, addiction, trauma—the list is endless. You will be dealing with people's fragile emotions, and they will hang onto every word you say.

Your primary objective is to help and heal. If the sitter isn't ready to hear something, don't force it. We are not here to cause pain or distress. Always give a positive message to take away from the reading. The world of Spirit is one of safety, love, and forgiveness. If someone is in true distress, connect them to a grief counselor or a suicide hotline. Maintain a list of professionals who can be of assistance in these cases. Your job is to be a healing presence. This might mean just sitting with someone for their time if they are not ready to hear from Spirit or feel unable to continue the reading. Their well-being always comes first. You are there to heal in whatever way you can offer.

You may have clients who have experienced great harm from the people that they are connecting to. They may have been neglected or abused; they may have been carrying the pain of their experiences with them for decades. It is not an easy thing to reconcile feelings for the person they loved with the person who also caused them great pain and suffering. They can have fear and anger, love and grief, side by side in their hearts. They are seeking closure, but they may also want to know that there is accountability.

I teach that we are all souls first who are having a human experience. We have come to Earth to learn many lessons for our soul's growth. Sometimes during that process, we get hurt, and conversely, we also hurt others. Once we pass on, we go through a life review in the Spirit world and see the pain that we caused others. We see if we took accountability for our actions and if we made amends. Typically, Spirits who didn't take responsibility while they were human will come through to acknowledge accountability and offer their apologies. You can help these souls, and your sitter, by conveying the apologies, and help your sitter to heal and move on from the pain. The world of Spirit brings the best and worst of humanity to you, and your mission is to help alleviate the pain and suffering of all concerned and break the cycles of trauma. This is deep soul work, in every sense of the meaning.

Being aware of the grief process is extremely important as it allows you to gauge where your client is emotionally. My rule of thumb is to always allow six months after the passing of a loved one before you hold a reading. This allows your client to go through the process of grieving. This is a soft rule that should be determined on a case-by-case basis. If you do a reading too soon after the deceased's passing, the client may not be emotionally ready. The reading takes on a different purpose: it's no longer about healing—it's about holding on. You have to be willing to say no if you know the client is not ready yet. Be kind, but firm, and offer to schedule a reading for them in the future.

I had a particular client who booked a reading with me. She was referred to me by a trusted client of mine. When I started the reading, it was clear to me that she was not in the best emotional state of mind. I had her husband in Spirit with me, and every time

I would say something, she would just cry. I asked how long it had been since his passing; she replied that it had been two months. It was no wonder that she was not in an emotional state to hear anything that I had to say. She wanted to hear from him so that she could hold onto him. After that reading, she tried to book me every other week. I had to tell her that it was unhealthy, and that she needed to complete the grieving process from his loss before I could do a reading for her again. It was a tough lesson for me to accept—I so wanted to help her with her loss, but had I continued, I would have done more harm than good.

In another situation, I had a mom who had lost her eighteen-year-old son in a car accident. She had waited a full six months before scheduling the reading; however, looking back on it, I probably should have had her wait longer. It was difficult for her to process the evidence I was bringing through. She cried during the entire reading, which prevented her from hearing me. Some details surrounding the accident were still too difficult and painful for her to confront. The reading began to lose its flow because I had to tend to her emotions.

These are just a couple of examples of situations that will happen to you. It's best to be prepared about how you will handle them, so you are able to make the right decisions in the moment.

I also have a rule about how frequently I will read for someone. Some clients can develop an addictive relationship to the medium or to the connection to Spirit. They want to schedule readings far too often, and for that reason, I have had to drop a client on occasion. Most people do well with a mediumship reading twice a year and a psychic reading once every couple of months, at most. Some people get readings every month and not much changes. You'll have to determine for yourself what you feel is healthy for your clients. You want to be a positive force in their lives, rather than a crutch. This guideline doesn't apply to practice readings or classes, where you are reaching out to hone your abilities. There is no harm in contacting Spirit multiple times, or doing frequent readings, in general. But if people approach you professionally and ask to book consecutive sessions close together, I recommend that they spread the sittings out to a frequency that can be the most beneficial.

As you continue down your path working as a medium, it is important for you to understand the seven stages of grief, so you can accurately assess the emotional state of your client:

Stage 1 - shock and denial (This is a state of disbelief and numbed feelings.)

Stage 2 - pain and guilt

Stage 3 - anger and bargaining

Stage 4 - depression

Stage 5 - the upward turn

Stage 6 - reconstruction and working through

Stage 7 - acceptance and hope

Grief will come in waves and will usually ebb and flow between different stages. In general, it's best to have readings later, rather than sooner, because grief is such a powerful emotion. People need time to process what's happened and deal with their loss before they can find healing and closure by connecting to Spirit. Keep in mind, everyone is different, and you need to judge for yourself where you feel a sitter is in the process.

If your sitter does become overwhelmed, give the person time for the emotions to settle before you proceed, and don't be afraid to wrap up a session early if it is too difficult. If you do stop a session early, it's important that you still give the message that Spirit wants to convey. Often, just telling people that you feel an overwhelming love, or that their loved one wants to comfort them, is enough to help them through their loss. Regardless, whatever feeling Spirit gives you that addresses their grief, pass that along, and hopefully it will help your sitters work through their losses.

You will also want to become a master wordsmith. Words have so much power, and they can mean different things to different people. Clients will hang onto every syllable you say, and some words can be harsh or offensive and will negatively impact your client. I cannot emphasize this enough: choose your words carefully. Words can be healing, but they can also hurt. We talked about triggers earlier, and how words can be powerful triggers for people. A descriptive word such as "addict," even though it may be completely accurate, might cause your sitter to become defensive and to shut down. The term "addict" may have a very negative connotation to them, whereas, if you were to say "substance abuse," that could be okay. With practice, you will learn how to phrase things to help your sitter hear the message and process what they need. You do not want to alienate them or cause them pain because of the words you choose.

I remember early on in my development, I was in a practice group on Facebook. There are a variety of practice groups where people post pictures of deceased loved ones so that emergent mediums can practice connecting to Spirit. These groups can be a great resource for you as you receive instant feedback on your connection and evidence. I had a particular instance that taught me a very valuable lesson. A woman posted a picture of her mother, who was in Spirit, and asked for people in the group to practice giving her a reading. I took my shot at it and wrote:

This lady is bitter. She has been hurt time and time again. She carries a chip on her shoulder. She could be very difficult to work with, and she struggles with relationships. She shields herself from others to protect her feelings. She was extremely protective of her kids, but also very strict and expected them to listen. On the other side, she is better at being relaxed and letting her guard down, but she still defends her actions as a sign of love. She did have a soft spot for animals; they couldn't hurt her.

How awful was that! I was not selective with my words at all. I said very few positive things about this lady's mother. Regardless if all of this was true or not, it was harsh, and not said with love or compassion. Whatever happens in the course of our lives, our souls, and the love we gave while on Earth, are beautiful and worthy. As a medium, you should always approach people, and the lives of those passed on, from a soul level—a place of generosity and kindness. Of course, the lady that had posted the picture reprimanded me, as she should have. To someone who is grieving the loss of a parent, hearing these words was hurtful. I cannot stress enough that you have to become a wordsmith. You will make mistakes but will learn from them. This is another reason why it is so important to practice on people we know. Luckily for me, this happened in a training/ practice group with a lady who was a medium herself, so she had experience with Spirit, and was forgiving of my mistakes.

If I were writing that now, I would say things very differently. I would lead with love and focus on the healing and connection in her story and write something more like this:

I have a lady who suffered greatly in her life. She didn't let a lot of people in emotionally; she protects her heart. Because of this, she may seem guarded and have difficulties in close personal relationships. She loved her kids and took much pride in protecting them. She was the disciplinarian in the household. She comes through today, saying how sorry she was for not showing more love; she can see now how she hurt her children. She could have done better.

Do you see the difference? I avoided negative words like "bitter" or "chip on her shoulder." I express empathy for her, and I focus on her strengths and positive traits. I convey her message of love for her children. I am offering the sitter a greater understanding, rather than putting them on the defensive. Sharing that she suffered, and protected her heart, can help them see why she may have been less loving than she could have been. Offering the takeaway that she loved them more fully and deeply than she was able to show could bring comfort to the sitter and allow healing to take place. It's the exact same connection and information from Spirit; the difference is in how I convey it, what I put in or leave out, and the words I use. Remember to always lead with love.

You will be talking about someone's family, loved one, or a person who was an important part of their lives. You certainly wouldn't want to hear someone close to you described that way, so don't use those words for someone else's loved one. Look for the kindest or most thoughtful way of saying everything. Focus on going deeper. Remember, when you get a piece of information from Spirit, pull three things from it and ask follow-up questions to flesh out more of the story. If someone's mother was hard to get close to, ask her when she felt closest to the sitter; when was a time she opened up? Dig deeper into the relationship.

Always keep kindness in mind when you're conveying the communication you receive. Phrase the information from a place of love. If their child died young, consider how a word like "reckless" might land on the ears of the parents. How would an adult child feel about your referring to a parent as "mean" or "bitter"? Aim for honesty, giving details in such a way that they understand the message, but so they don't feel that you're judging them or their loved one. You might say the person in Spirit "took risks" or "could be difficult," but make sure you go deep enough to find positives as well, perhaps their love of life, or that they were a good provider. Balance the good and bad and use words in a way that is comforting as well as true.

There are some words you want to avoid entirely because they can be very painful for a lot of people. Substitute more thoughtful and compassionate words when you can.

Some examples of word use:

- dead/died - passed
- dying - transitioning
- drug abuse - substance abuse
- alcoholic - substance abuse pertaining to alcohol
- killed themselves/suicide - took responsibility for their passing

Always lead with compassion. Read body language. If the reading is getting tough for your sitter, stop and allow them to gather themselves. Their emotional and mental state is your number one priority. What we do is sacred. We have to have empathy and compassion.

Unless you are a trained medical doctor, refrain from giving any type of medical advice, diagnosis, treatment, etc. This type of information could be misconstrued. If a client tells you about a medical condition or symptoms, refer the sitter to a medical professional. Again, be honest. If you're getting something from Spirit related to health, indicate you're not sure what this is referring to, but suggest seeing a doctor. You don't want to scare anyone, so keep it light and brief. Your job is spiritual, not physical.

The same applies to clients with mental illness or suicidal tendencies. You are not a trained and licensed counselor. Always refer your client to a medical professional or therapist. Put together a resource list of medical and mental health professionals as a part of your business. Investigate local outreach and suicide hotline numbers, hospitals, etc. You want people to get the help they need.

Last, I want to give you the Lisa Williams Code of Ethics, which I think provides a good framework for the work we do. Beyond that, just keep in mind that we are healers, and always approach your clients with honesty, kindness, and love. You are here to help people through some of the most difficult pain they will ever know. But with help from Spirit, you can also give them some of the greatest healing they will ever experience. And that's when the true power of the work we've chosen to do reveals itself. Happy healing.

LWISSD (Lisa Williams International School of Development) Code of Ethics:

- Be respectful, compassionate, and kind. You are carrying your clients', students', and colleagues' emotional well-being in your hands, especially when delivering difficult information.
- Be respectful and kind to your teachers, other students, colleagues, and staff.
- Be respectful of your abilities, as it is a gift from God, and it should not be used as a "party trick."
- Be respectful of the gifts of other psychics, mediums, and healers.
- Be in integrity with all that you do and only use your gift for the highest good of others.
- Be truthful no matter how hard it is and speak from your heart.
- Ensure that you leave your client with hope and an understanding of the afterlife.
- Practice, promote, and adhere to spiritual ethics in all that you do.

- Agree not to discriminate on the basis of gender, ethnicity, religious beliefs, age, physical disabilities, and culture.
- Always gain insight and knowledge from your connection with Spirit, and never ask too many questions of the client. Researching clients prior to a reading is a school infraction and will result in expulsion.
- Always gain written permission from others when sharing a personal story from a reading or a picture for (and not limited to) social media, published articles, books, and websites.
- Never allow a client to lead your reading with too much information or by telling them what they want to hear.
- Never let your ego get in the way. Should you not make the connection with Spirit, close the reading and, if money has been exchanged, refund the fee.
- Remember to always thank Spirit, and your client, for enabling the connection, as it is an honor and privilege to serve Spirit.
- Remember positivity creates positivity (Law of Attraction).
- Understand that anything is possible and believe in yourself.

CHAPTER ELEVEN

THE PERSONAL JOURNEY OF MEDIUMSHIP

Believe in your infinite potential. Your only limitations are those
you set upon yourself.
-Roy T. Bennett

I began the preface of this book with a quote from John Holland: *"Your gifts are like a rose unfolding. You cannot force the bloom. When the rose is opened, then and only then, will you see it, feel it, and finally know it."*

As I reflect back from where I started, that quote is even more powerful for me than ever before. I don't believe that people can just wake up one day and declare themselves a medium. It truly is a journey with a beginning and an end. It includes everything that happens in between: all the experiences that mold you and that offer you growth, understanding, knowledge, wisdom, patience, compassion, and the most significant gift of them all—truth.

We are each a blooming rose. We need to nurture the gift, feed it, embrace it, and enjoy its beauty. Each petal is a different lesson being presented to us—one at a time. And if we don't learn the lessons the first time, Spirit will show us again through another experience.

I promised myself when I started documenting this journey that I would include everything—the good, the bad, and the ugly. I have taken six steps ahead in my confidence only to take five steps back. Everyone looking in from the outside thinks, "What a gift to have!" However, they have no idea of the responsibility that weighs on a medium, and the amount of work and perseverance that it takes to become a good one. Many tears have been shed, and many days I have wanted to give up. There were so many fears that came up that I had to fight through and overcome. However, these pale in comparison to the number of hearts that I have touched.

I want to share with you in this chapter some of the difficulties I've faced, mistakes I've made, and lessons I've learned. My hope is that showing you the path I've walked will make your road a little easier. My prayer is that you walk your path with confidence and joy whenever possible, and always with the knowledge that you are worthy of the task, and not alone.

Fear

During this journey, you may question your gifts on many occasions. You may often feel as if you will never be good enough. Spirit has given you the ability to trust in yourself unconditionally—know that you are good enough. This is why self-healing is so important on your journey. Believe in yourself, or no one else will. We each have the power to revise the story that we have been told all our lives or that we have told ourselves.

Fear will be the most common thing that will keep you from reaching your true potential. You are meant to be greater than you are; don't let fear keep you stagnant or stuck. You must push through your fear and move beyond your comfort zone in order to truly succeed.

Everyone embarking on a mediumship journey will have different goals and purposes. Don't compare yourself to anyone else. This is your very own personalized journey, taken at your own individual pace. Every time you do something you didn't think you could do, you will become a little more confident. Your world will become a little bigger, and your fear a little smaller. Step by step, you walk this path. Every time you find yourself stopped by fear, remember that your potential, and your reason for doing this, is greater than any fear that you might feel. Your job is to live up to your soul's calling and be a light in the world, and to walk through the doors that Spirit opens for you.

Learning to Surrender

A really difficult lesson on this journey of mine has been acknowledging that I am not in control of the process. The Spirit world has its own agenda. I am merely the vessel by which to deliver the messages. This was a very hard lesson for me to get, one that almost caused me to give up on my journey. But thankfully, Spirit pushed me to see it through, and I am so glad I did. The following story is an account of how two roads were presented to me, and how I chose which one to take.

Robin is a wonderful woman who does my landscaping along with her husband, and early in my journey she became a critical part of my growth. Why? Because she pushed me to give readings! Robin wouldn't take "no" for an answer. I gave in, and we set up two readings in one day with friends of hers. The first one would be with a man, and later that afternoon, there would be a reading with his cousin. It's important to know they were related. This was going to be my first attempt to give an actual reading to someone that I didn't know. I was very nervous going in. I sat in the car for about twenty minutes preparing to get into the zone. I was picking up very strong feelings of a lady in Spirit that was with me. I just knew that this reading was going to be about this very lovely lady. I then went in and sat down to do the reading. Robin was there with me for support.

The man came in and sat down, and I proceeded to try and make my link. I began to describe the lady that I had with me in Spirit. He did not recognize her. I asked him if his mother had crossed over. He replied with a no. I then did something that you are not supposed to do—I asked him who he was hoping to connect with. He told me that he wanted to connect with his father who had passed away when he was younger. I then try to "summon" his father to talk to me. I was getting nothing on him. What I saw instead were images in my mind of this woman. I just could not shake her. Spirit suggested I ask this woman to step aside and allow the man's father to come through. And that is what I did.

When I described the woman again, he said it sounded like his aunt, but he really wanted to hear from his father. I tried again and again, and I just wasn't getting anything! I was devastated; I apologized to the man, and we ended the session. I just went back to my car and cried. This was still early in my journey, and to have had such a failure on my first official reading was too much for me to accept. I didn't know what to do; I was questioning everything. Maybe I wasn't meant to do this. Maybe I am not a medium. Maybe this has been all a waste of time. I had this thought: "I am done!"

Now remember, I had scheduled another reading that evening with his cousin. I was just sick to my stomach at the thought of going through the same scenario with her. I spent the remainder of the day wanting to call the cousin and cancel the reading! This is where the path diverges. I could have given in to my fear, given up on my abilities, and just walked away from mediumship. My first reading had been a disaster, my confidence was shot, and I was scared to death of ever trying again. I was ready to throw in the towel. The only reason I didn't quit is because I had felt the female Spirit's energy so intensely all day long. I felt in my gut that I just had to do this reading, and that this Spirit had something she really wanted to say. I went to lie down and get in the proper mindset about a half-hour before my client was scheduled to arrive. I took a notebook with me and just started writing everything that came to mind.

When my client and my (still) very supportive landscaper arrived, we all sat down. At this point, I just told myself to trust what I got and just go for it, so I did! Without hesitation or restraint, I just surrendered and shared everything that was coming to me. My client sat there a little bit bewildered. She had never been to a medium before. I couldn't tell if I was getting everything right, or if she thought I was crazy. Well, I was getting it all right! I had the pleasure of bringing forth her mother, who was the aunt of the gentleman I had read earlier. Mom definitely wanted her message heard! As for me . . . well, point taken, Spirit world! I realized that I can't force a Spirit to appear, and I can't dictate the terms of the connection, or which direction the messages take me; I can only accept and convey what Spirit gives me, just letting Spirit take the wheel.

That episode was a great lesson to me about surrendering. One failure did not signify the end of my journey. My pain was irrelevant. If I got things wrong, I got things wrong. I had to learn to let go and keep going. It's not about you or me, it's about the Spirit world. Allow the Spirits you bring in to lead the way for you.

Highs and Lows of Mediumship

Eventually, I reached a place where my confidence in my abilities had grown considerably. I had been receiving an abundance of messages from Spirit, and a lot of validation from them. I was starting to get really excited about the direction that my journey was going in. I had come out of the psychic closet—no more hiding who I am and what I do. I was gaining confidence and starting to see the results of the work that I had put in.

Every other Saturday, I attended a psychic development class, followed immediately by a mediumship development class. Due to my schedule, I only had these two days every month to practice and develop my skills, so when those days arrived, I got really excited. Well, on this occasion, Spirit had an extra special lesson planned for me!

The start of the psychic development class was no different than any other time I had attended. We usually started with a meditation so that we could all get into an altered state. This meditation, however, was different. Instead of meeting a guide who gave me a message, I was greeted by a young boy. I had never been interrupted during a meditation by someone in Spirit. The experience with him was a little surreal. He held my hand, and we ran through fields, and he carried a small truck in his hand. I spent the whole meditation getting to know him. On Earth, he was sick. He had an illness for a long time, but he was showing me that he was okay. He was playing and laughing with me. I knew that this little boy must belong to someone in the class.

In my mind, he was a little reddish-blond-haired boy with freckles who had cancer and passed away. He wanted to let someone know he was fine, and that he didn't want them to be sad anymore. Right away, I became fixated on details like hair color that might not have been right. There was a new man that had come to class that day, and I felt a very strong attraction to him. He was in great turmoil emotionally. (I am an empath and can feel other people's emotions.) My mind jumps in to tell me that this little boy must belong to him because he also had reddish-blonde hair. I was almost certain that I had drawn the right conclusion. He and I were put together during class to work on a psychic exercise together. I drew up the courage to ask him if he, or anyone he had known, had lost a little red-headed boy. He sat and thought for a moment and said, "No." I couldn't believe his response. "Really?" I was sure that the boy was his. My brain had told me it had to be for him. At that point, I had lost all focus. How could I have been so sure about something like that and had it turn out not to be true?

The psychic class ended, and the mediumship development class was about to start. The man I had been focused on stayed for the next class. I sat in the corner of the room still trying to figure out where I had gone wrong. I saw everything in my mind. It had taken me months to trust what I see. Could I have just imagined this little boy? I was determined to figure it out.

During class we all took turns standing up and connecting with someone's loved one on the other side. When it was my turn, I continued to focus on this man. I should have let go and trusted what I was getting and asked to see if anyone else in the room could relate. Instead, I continued to believe that the little boy belonged to him. He had told me earlier that his mom had passed away when he was in his late twenties. So, I let my mind create the scenario that maybe his mom was the one connecting with me and was trying to show me this man as a child, and that she was the one who was actually sick. I was letting my left brain take over and was trying to force things—everything that I've told you not to do! I felt utterly defeated and eventually gave up.

Another student stood up for her turn to connect with a Spirit and the first thing she said was, "I have a little boy here, maybe seven years old." She went on to say, "There is definitely a little boy. Has anyone lost a son?" I looked around the room and couldn't believe it. One of the new students was nodding her head, with the caveat that the age didn't fit. I was dumbfounded. Was that the same little boy that I had seen in my meditation? I sat and listened as the reading was being given and was unsure. This was a development class, so not a lot of detail was required. The reader said that daisies were significant somehow, and she mentioned something about a high school. It wasn't until she gave the message as to why the boy was here that I *knew* that was my little boy. The message to his mom was "I don't want you to be sad anymore," the exact same message that my little boy gave me to deliver. The boy's mom was there. I couldn't believe that I got it all so wrong! Why did I continue to focus on the wrong person even after I found out that the message wasn't for him? Why did I translate a long illness to cancer? You see, this mom lost her thirteen-year-old son to a heart attack while he was at baseball camp.

How did I get it all completely wrong? How could I let this beautiful Spirit down, and more importantly, let down his mom? What if she'd never received his message? I went home unable to shake the experience. I hardly slept that night, replaying in my mind exactly where I went wrong. I chose to be alone the next day to sort it all out. I knew there had to be a valuable lesson here.

After playing hermit, and shedding some tears, I was able to look back and see what went wrong. I was too literal with the details of what I was seeing. I let my left brain step in and complete the story. I tried to force something and gave up. The man's "no" didn't mean I was wrong—it meant that the interpretation that I made was wrong. I should have pushed through it; I shouldn't have been so focused on the details being exactly right. I allowed my brain to get in the way and overthink it. Regardless of that experience, I was determined not to let that one experience defeat me.

Mistakes like this one are about learning and growing, and that experience taught me plenty. It allowed me to see that I was truly a medium!

Spirit gave me an opportunity that weekend to overcome and correct the mistake. I almost allowed myself to repeat that same mistake. Almost! If you don't get it right the first time, Spirit will give you the lesson again, until you get it right.

I sometimes started picking up information from Spirit before the class even began. The following occurrence is just one example of this. As I was leaving home for the class, I just started crying, for no apparent reason. I thought to myself that this was going to be an emotional class. We were running a little late, so my daughter Jazmine offered to drive because she thought she could get there faster than her slow-driving mama! I graciously agreed, so I could spend the car ride in a light meditation to prepare for the class.

In my head, a story started developing. I was visualizing the hand of a man who seemed to be of an advanced age. Then I saw one single jingle bell, which quickly turned into an entire row of bells. I got the feeling that these bells hung on a door, and that this older gentleman got quite annoyed with them, in a humorous kind of way. He then showed me a garden. At that moment, I felt the same sadness that I had felt earlier. I thought that he was showing me his wife's grief. I saw a small white cat and then the message came: "I will be here waiting for you, but take your time. You have a lot of life to live and people still need you." And that was all there was.

I turned to my daughter who was driving and told her this amazing story I had just received. Based on past history, I decided to trust that what I had just seen was Spirit communicating with me. But then there comes the part when my brain takes over. The gentleman was older, and the message was for his wife. If this message was from Spirit, I should expect to find an older lady in our class today who is meant to hear it, right?

We got to class, and yes, we were terribly late. Traffic was horrible! We walked in and my teacher and one other regular student were the only people there. I knew for certain that the person there had not lost a husband. Sigh . . . maybe it was my imagination and not Spirit after all. About twenty minutes went by in class, and we were doing some medium exercises when someone knocked on the door. A brand-new student walked in, apologizing for being late. Her GPS had taken her on an adventure. The woman was my age, and through conversation, I learned she was married, but not to the person I was looking for. Now I was really confused. Then it was my turn to get up, connect with Spirit, and give a reading. I was uncertain about whether to forget everything I had gotten on the car ride, since it apparently didn't fit, or just trust Spirit and say what I saw.

Well, I had learned my lesson. I chose the latter. I stood up and said that I was not 100% sure who my message would be for. I had an older gentleman who presented himself to me as a husband. I went on to describe the bells on the door and his annoyance with them, because they prevented him from sneaking in at night. I heard a gasp come from the side of the room, and it was the new student. She confirmed that it was her dad. Her mother had hung the bells on the doorknob so that every time he would get home late, those darn bells would wake her up! I went on to deliver the other information I had received, and the great sadness I had felt. His wife was still hurting badly. I came to find out that his death was quite recent, and that she was having a very difficult time emotionally. It was a beautiful experience, filled with lots of tears.

It wasn't until days later, as I reflected on that experience, that I realized exactly the lessons Spirit was teaching me. Watch out for stereotypes. Don't assume anything or let your mind get in the way. Give what's being given. Trust the process. Spirit is smarter than I am. If I am getting a message, it's because Spirit knows that the right person will show up! I am the student, and the Spirits are my teachers.

Understanding this is how each of us as mediums are able to bloom.

Crossing Boundaries: When Mediumship Interferes with Your Personal Life

Communications from Spirit started to become much more frequent for me, and they expanded beyond the classroom or practice groups. I have now started to get messages from Spirit at random times and for people I hadn't expected. With this growth comes internal conflicts that I have to face. In a classroom environment, everyone is there for the same purpose, and they all have a similar belief system regarding the metaphysical. However, once Spirit decided it was time for me to work with them, I have had to deal with people who think I'm a fake, or crazy, or in cahoots with the devil himself. I have learned to ignore negativity online and not give it any attention. Everyone will have an opinion, and it is not your job to try and change it. What people say online is none of my business, but what happens in my real life is a different story.

I often feel the isolation that this gift can bring. I have become hypersensitive, and my feelings are easily hurt. I live between my spiritual world and my mainstream life. In the spiritual realm, I feel safe to be me, but I struggle at times in the mainstream world with who I am now. Situations occur when I'm with my mainstream friends and I get a message from their loved one. I have to carefully consider the different possibilities: "Do I share it? What if I freak them out? What if they start withdrawing from me? What if that same fear causes me to withdraw from them?"

Because of my hypersensitivity to energy, I sometimes avoid going out in public. I can't tell you how many times I've gone to the grocery store and just sat in the parking lot, unable to go in. Wide open spaces and large numbers of people can at times challenge me. I think to myself that this can't be good. I am still learning how to walk this part of my journey—how to be open and vulnerable to everything that Spirit wants to share with me while still enjoying the beautiful chaos of this life while I'm in the midst of it. I guess this is a part of the journey called "growing pains!"

Since my crazy journey began and my gifts were awakened, I've gone through many different stages. I miss the naïve, excited, curious, and oblivious person I was early on before I recognized my gift. I'm now at that part of my journey where I know that not everyone believes in what I experience or even wants to hear about it. Not everyone finds it exciting and magical, and not everyone wants to connect with a loved one who has crossed over.

I was faced with this very issue on my way to class one day. As I was driving in my car, I started to receive messages. When this happens, I never know if I'll get just a brief message or a longer, more detailed one. This time, Spirit made a very good connection and told me this story. I had to pull over as quickly as possible so I could write it down. Here is the message as it was told to me:

"I am an uncle. Big, burly guy with a beard who loved the outdoors. I had an accident, but I didn't die at that time. I died later, but it was related to the accident. My wife suffered after my death. She died of a broken heart. My death sparked a domino effect for her, one death after another, in a short amount of time." I felt his wife with him. But he did all the talking. He was her strength. Then I was given these images: a domino, a swatch of a pink baby blanket, Disney's *Beauty and the Beast*, and the names Laurie and Maddison. A message of gratitude was Spirit's closing thought.

Once I received the name Laurie, I was taken aback for a second. I had just recently started communicating with my daughter-in-law's stepmom, Shelly. Earlier that week, we had our first-ever real conversation, and I got to know her a little bit. I vaguely remembered her mentioning her sister, Laurie, who had passed away about four months earlier. Could it be? Was the man who came to me in Spirit my daughter-in-law's uncle? Whoa! I barely knew these people; but what I did know was that they are strict Christians! I couldn't go to her with this. She would have thought I was crazy!

All this happened right before class, mind you, so I had plenty of time to stew on it. During class, we practice giving each other readings. The person who was paired up with me, not knowing anything about what was going on in my head that day, said these magic words: "Just deliver the message and don't worry about what they think of you."

Taking the advice that I had been given, after class I messaged Shelly. "Didn't you say your sister's name was Laurie?" She replied, "Yes, why?" And so it began. Prefacing the message with "You may think I'm crazy, but . . . .", I then delivered the message I had received and the images that were given to me. She was not sure what to think of it all. Her Christian beliefs told her that this was wrong, and that one should not seek out spiritual mediums. However, she felt the need to take in the information, and she replied to me with her story, along with a picture of her sister with a big, burly guy with a beard.

About ten or fifteen years ago, the brother of her sister's friend was shot in the back and ended up paralyzed. Three years ago, her sister became his caretaker, and they developed a romantic relationship. She was his legs, and he was her brain (she had suffered an aneurysm years ago and suffered from memory loss). He had to have surgery and ended up passing away. The medical examiner officially stated that his death was related to his original injuries. Four weeks later, her sister died of a spontaneous tear in the heart (literally, a broken heart). A few months later, her uncle passed away (making it three deaths within a three-month span). After that death, her uncle's neighbor was caught breaking into the house trying to steal his dominos. Her all-time favorite Disney movie was *Beauty and the Beast*. Her sister left behind two teenage girls, one of whom is pregnant and leaning towards naming her baby Addison, which was close to the Maddison name I had been given. The other daughter had put a piece of her pink baby blanket in with her mother.

"Just deliver the message," Spirit said. "Leave the rest in our hands." I didn't want to pass on that message because I didn't want to bring my mediumship into a family that didn't believe in psychics, or even ask for connection, but Spirit had other plans. I believe that I am here to do what Spirit asks of me, and I need to trust that it is the right thing to do. Spirit is always asking more of me than I feel ready to give. Every time this has happened, I found that Spirit has always had my back.

Another major boundary I am dealing with right now is work. I also have a mainstream career. I am in sales, and I have been with my company for almost twenty years. I am the sole provider in my home. A couple of weeks ago, I ran into my ex-husband, and he had some words of advice to give me: "You shouldn't post any of this medium stuff online or tell anyone at work about it, or you could lose your job."

I could actually lose my twenty-year career because dead people talk to me? Now that was a reality check for me. I never would have even considered that to be possible. It probably isn't, but if there are people out there who believe that, then that makes it a possibility! What was I supposed to do—live a secret life, remove all work-related friends from my social media pages, and isolate even more?

I have done some soul-searching. While I am knowledgeable about the world around me, it doesn't mean I have to live my life in fear of it. This is who I am—the person that Spirit chose to work with them. This is their rodeo; I chose to get on for the ride.

Spirit obviously sees no boundaries between my personal life and my business life, and when there is a message to be delivered, they can be very persistent. I was sitting in a large conference room listening to a training presentation with some of my co-workers. While everyone else was jotting down notes, I was writing down messages that I was receiving from a mom in Spirit. Back then, there was no way I was telling anyone at work what I was experiencing (except two close friends I trusted). So, I jotted down my "notes" and just kept them all to myself. Secretly, I was dying to ask someone about the message, just so I could validate what I was getting, but not enough to reveal myself to my management team. That experience with the mom in Spirit stayed with me. I was never able to just let it go and move on. I just knew in my gut it was meant for someone in that room that day.

Fast forward a few months to December and our office Christmas lunch. The night before, I was feeling the presence of Spirit, and the only thing I heard was the name Susan. I do not know any Susan that had crossed over, so I just brushed it off as my imagination. The next morning while I was getting ready for our luncheon, I had the memory of the mom who was with me in the conference room back in October. Back on that day, the one thing that stood out the most was a Raggedy Ann doll she was showing me. A few minutes later, my co-worker with whom I had confided in, sent me a text message. She had found out the name of another co-worker's mom who had passed away a few years back. The co-worker who had lost her mother was hoping I would be able to connect with her mother for her. In her text, she wrote: "Her mom's name was Susan." I was taken aback and wondered, am I ready to cross over and mix my personal life with my business world? At that point, I did not think I had a choice. This mother obviously wants her daughter to know that she is around. She had been trying to get my attention for months!

So, I did it. I broke through the boundary. I shared with her the story of the day back in the conference room. The Raggedy Ann doll was a huge reference for her and validation for both of us. Now, because yet another person had overheard the conversation at the Christmas party, my close circle of two people at work knowing about my mediumship had grown to a whopping four. Baby steps—it's true, but it was only a matter of time before it spread like wildfire. Hopefully, I don't get in trouble with my job. In any event, I accept it as all part of the gig I signed up for before I was born.

I have to trust that God and Spirit know what they are doing, and I will have to surrender to the fact that I am a medium. I am not going to force messages on anyone, but I have to trust that I will only be given the messages that are meant to be received. I have to trust that my role here on Earth includes more than my career, and people are more open than my fears might say they are. Because of everything that's happened in my life, trust can be hard for me, even with Spirit. I am still learning to let go and know the Universe will catch me if I fall. But every time I honor Spirit's request to step forward into the unknown, I've found that the path appears beneath my feet. I continue to learn and trust more with every step.

Every time you connect to Spirit, it's a learning experience and an opportunity for growth. Every decision you make to be open or kind, to choose trust and healing, is a step on your path. You will make mistakes. You will miss messages or misinterpret information. You're human. You will stray from the path and have to start over again. There is simply no way to learn and grow that doesn't involve failing or falling down and having to get back up again. Your journey as a medium only stops on the day you decide it's not for you. Just try your best, continue to learn as much as you can, and you will cultivate your gift fully, beautifully.

Let your rose bloom.

CHAPTER TWELVE

THERE IS PURPOSE IN YOUR PAIN

You must first walk through the storm to experience the rainbow.
-Tracey Escobar

You may find this chapter somewhat triggering at first—and that's okay.

Whenever we are asked to look at ourselves in the mirror and evaluate our actions and reactions, it can feel very uncomfortable. However, if you want to make significant changes in your life, you must look at the role you play in every interaction and make the necessary adjustments to *self*. Remember, you are the only person whose attitude and perspective you can control.

Perspective is how we view the world and ourselves through our life-experience lens. We can view ourselves as a victim of the circumstances in our lives, or we can be empowered by them. The choice is up to you. Notice the difference in the tone of the first statement below and that of the second. Which one is more empowered, and which is more empowering?

- "Bad things always happen to me."
- "When things are not going as I hoped or planned in my life, I trust that it's for my growth and highest good."

Victim Mentality

Victim mentality is an acquired personality trait in which people consider themselves victims of the negative actions of others. Even in the face of contrary evidence, a victim behaves as if this were the case. In some cases, people with a victim mentality have, in fact, been the victim of wrongdoing by others, or have otherwise suffered misfortune through no fault of their own. However, such misfortune does not necessarily imply that one will respond by developing a pervasive and universal victim mentality.

These are the traits people adopt when they choose a victim mentality:

- They do not take responsibility for their own life.
- They are not accountable for their own actions and reactions.
- They need others to solve their problems for them.
- Their story has become their identity.
- They are addicted to drama in life.
- They blame others for the way their life is.
- They think life is working against them.
- They have trouble coping with problems and feel powerless.
- They feel stuck and approach things with a negative attitude.

Living Empowered

To be empowered means to reclaim the power of your natural self.

Empowerment is not something that can be given to you by someone else. Our power is fully contained within ourselves, and it is our job to accept full responsibility for it.

Empowered traits include:

- responsibility and accountability for your own actions and reactions.
- self-awareness.
- self-reflection.
- optimism.
- wholeness.
- peace.
- trust.
- confidence.
- meaningful connections.
- gratitude.
- abundance.

Shifting your mindset will change your life. Is it easy? No, nothing worthwhile ever is. Is it a necessary step to becoming a medium? Yes, it is very necessary in your work as a medium.

Victim mentality is low-vibrational. If you stay stuck in the lower vibrations, you will attract lower vibrational energy. Your job is to raise your own vibration so that you can be the beacon of light for others. The Spirit world is of the highest vibration known—that of unconditional love. In order to be of service to the Spirit realm, you have to see through the lens of Spirit by cultivating a deep understanding about soul lessons. These are lessons in acceptance, understanding, compassion, empathy, and unconditional love.

Life and Its Lessons Continue

As we walk this Earth plane, life continues to provide obstacles, hurt, pain, and suffering. It also provides us opportunities for growth, happiness, gratitude, and empowerment. The difference, when you reach the other side of healing, is your perspective, mindset, and attitude. With our growth comes the ability to see the blessings in the lessons.

During 2019 and 2020, I confronted several major challenges. It was as if the Universe was testing me to see how much I had truly progressed in all the years I had worked so hard to create a life in harmony with Spirit. Could I keep my vibration high even through additional trauma? Could I continue to practice what I was teaching others? Could I truly find the blessing in every lesson?

A period of loss and release began in July of 2019 when my boyfriend's "old classmate" began following me on Instagram when he told her that he had "a former girlfriend" who was a medium. She had recently lost her dad and was curious about my work. While she was learning more about me, she saw one of my posts about a lovely weekend I spent picking blueberries. She saw the picture and remembered that her old classmate, who she now had a "friend-with-benefits" relationship with, had told her that he was going to a blueberry farm with his cousin that same weekend. Curious, she wondered if I was more than just an "old girlfriend."

At that point, she decided to reach out to me and book a reading. I decided to meet her for dinner and a reading at a local Mexican restaurant. She was an old friend of my boyfriend, so of course, I wanted to give her special treatment. When she met me for the reading, she was very sweet, even vulnerable, with big brown eyes, long hair braided behind her. As I read for her, I felt something was not right. She veered off the subject of her father, wanting to talk about her love life. It didn't take long for me to realize that there was something more to her relationship with my boyfriend of fifteen years. After some prodding, I discovered that she had been having a friends-with-benefits relationship with my boyfriend for a year-and-a-half! She then shared everything with me about their love affair. I was shocked and heartbroken. That experience would change the course of my life and completely turn my world upside down.

I dealt with it by accepting a job opportunity several states away in North Carolina. By October of 2019, I had left my job, my home, my children, and grandchildren to start over again. I had a really difficult time breaking off the relationship, so I stayed in it. I ended up traveling back and forth between North Carolina and Texas while trying to mend a relationship with someone I knew I could not trust. I was codependent and addicted to what I perceived at the time as a passionate love.

By December, I was still traveling between the two states trying to save my relationship, and then my dog, Hurley, was diagnosed with cancer. I paid for surgery to try and save his life. I was managing the dog's illness from North Carolina while relying on my son to take care of him in Texas. Despite the surgery, the tumor grew back, and I had to have him put down.

Then in January, I received a call that one of my closest friends, Valerie, was in the emergency room at a hospital in Dallas. Valerie had been care-flighted from a small town in Texas. She was a vibrant woman in her forties who had always been healthy except for a minor thyroid-related issue. She had become very ill over the Christmas holidays, but thought it was the flu. She was starting to feel better; then one day, she sat up in bed, her eyes rolled back, and she just collapsed. Her husband did CPR until the ambulance and Care Flight arrived, trying to save her life. My dear friend suffered a major cardiac arrest.

When I arrived at the hospital, her eyes were vacant, and the only signs of life were twitches that ran throughout her pale, fragile body. The drip-drip of IVs, the blinking of screens, tubes, and wires kept her alive. Within several days they pronounced her brain-dead. (We think now it may have been Covid-19.)

Valerie came to me in a vision. I remember having to go to the hospital that Saturday morning, before they pronounced her completely gone. I was lying in bed with my eyes closed and saw people in motion like a black-and-white movie. And then, Valerie showed up in the movie. She was getting out of her hospital bed and putting on her jeans and T-shirt. She pulled her hair to the side, looked at me, then turned and walked away. And right at that moment, I knew that she was going to die. Dealing with Valerie's death was my first personal loss since my mediumship journey began, and it was a much different experience than my dad's passing was. I was very sad that she was gone, but I took comfort in knowing where she went.

The whole time she was in the hospital on life support, whenever her favorite songs would play on the radio, it was as if she were speaking with me telepathically. Nickelback's "Photograph" aired repeatedly wherever I went, like a mantra throughout the last days and hours of her life:

I had the photo album spread out on my bedroom floor
It's hard to say it, time to say it
Goodbye, goodbye It's hard to say it,
Time to say it
Goodbye, goodbye

Her favorite songs offered a magical backdrop to a difficult, unexpected loss. Lyrics, such as "Memories," by Maroon 5, connected me to her as she was suspended between the worlds:

Toast to the ones here today
Toast to the ones that we lost on the way
'Cause the drinks bring back all the memories
And the memories bring back, memories bring back you

A few months before she died, Valerie told me, "Tracey. You have to leave your boyfriend. That is when everything will change for you. When you leave him, your career as a medium will suddenly take off . . . ." I was taken back with her prediction and thought, "What does my relationship have to do with my mediumship career?" I blew it off at the moment, but I also knew Valerie had a keen intuition. It turns out that, indeed, she was right.

I was still flying back and forth between North Carolina and Texas. When the Covid epidemic erupted, suddenly all my travel halted. The world went into lockdown. I was then living in a house all by myself, isolated. That's when the depression hit me out of nowhere. I hadn't really suffered from depression since my awakening back in 2016. By 2020, I was off all my medications, so it came out of the blue and struck me hard—I never even saw it coming. One day I was fine, and the next day I was holding on to dear life to stay alive.

In the past, my depression was always accompanied by suicidal thoughts, but they were just passing thoughts. This time was different. The thoughts were real, and I was struggling to survive every minute, day, and night during one of the longest weeks of my life.

"Can I get through this?" I wondered, with the heaviness of my heart, as each day I lost the desire to live. "In a past life, I probably did take my life." Perhaps the lesson was to see if I could push past the all-consuming pain to see that it was temporary. I don't remember everything that I went through during those five or six days, but I woke up one morning and the depression was completely gone without medication or therapy. I survived a week in time when I lost my mind.

What was the lesson for me in that suffering? Maybe it was about my ability to survive the depression, knowing all that I know now—that feelings are often fleeting. Maybe it was Spirit teaching me to have more compassion towards those who commit suicide, so I could explain to loved ones the depth of suffering that can lead to suicide.

Since then, many clients have reached out to me with stories of suicides committed by their beloveds. I have a better understanding now of suicide, and I can counsel them more effectively. Last week, I had a suicide reading. I told the sitter, "Spirit tells me that contemplating suicide is as if you're drowning, and you can't come up for air."

And she said, "Oh, my God, that's exactly how he explained it."

Now, looking back, I do see the purpose in the pain. However, at the time, it was not quite so clear.

During this same time, I was depressed and probably the most vulnerable I had been in a long time. My oldest daughter Jazmine shared with me that she had had mommy issues for most of her twenty-nine years. She explained how she had never felt seen, loved, or heard by me. She even used the term "narcissist" to describe me. I was definitely taken back by the revelation. I had no idea she had ever felt that way or that I had done things to make her feel like this. I realized that there was a lesson in her communication, but I wasn't ready to hear it because the message was painful. I already felt horrible and wanted to die. And now, I learn that I have deeply hurt my oldest child.

At first, I got very defensive—I am human. "I have no idea what you are talking about. I gave you the best of everything I could." From my perspective, I loved as hard as I could, and I did the very best I knew how to do at the time. But if I were to be completely honest with myself, I raised three kids while in survival mode. I was in a constant state of fight-or-flight.

Naturally, her reality clashed against mine. I sat with everything she told me. I would replay that conversation over and over again in my mind. How could I have gone so wrong?

Once I got over the depression, I did all I could to mend our relationship. I wrote her letters, gave her gifts, and was careful of what I said to her to avoid any disagreement or misunderstanding. Even though my intent wasn't ever to hurt her, sometimes I would say things that she would interpret in a hurtful manner. Our relationship became strained and complicated.

About the same time, my company let me come back to Texas for the next year. I put everything in storage in North Carolina, got in my car, and drove back home.

By August of 2020, I was changing. My perspective on my relationship with my boyfriend was changing. I was constantly being triggered in that relationship. Everything was starting to make me angry. I had a text message conversation with him that led to an argument. He usually was the one to reach out when we fought. This time, he didn't. That became my opportunity to finally walk away from the relationship. As long as he didn't reach out, I was finally ready to let the relationship go.

We haven't spoken since that last text message. I had finally come to realize the reality of the situation. We couldn't progress as a couple because of all the things holding him back from loving me fully. His traumas. His own prison. I can thank him now for letting me go and finally giving me the opportunity to have a normal life and a full-time, committed love that I really longed for, but that realization and gratitude came months and months into healing from the trauma this relationship caused me.

Fast forward to a week before Thanksgiving, Jazmine called me, and we got into a disagreement over some recent family issues. I had been struggling most of 2020 and I was grieving so much loss that I failed to hear her—to really hear what she was trying to tell me behind her anger and hurt. In retrospect, I realize now that I was in my own pain and not in a place to hear hers.

Jasmine eventually hung up on me, then immediately sent out a family text message to cancel her participation in Thanksgiving and the thirtieth-birthday party that I was organizing for her. She was done—with me.

I wished I could have maintained a higher perspective, but I am human, and all I could do was forgive myself for my reaction, with the hope that one day Jazmine might also forgive me. Her wounds run deep, and this build-up of negative emotions was years and years in the making. Our relationship is completely damaged and may never be reconciled. I am now part of the Estranged Parents Club, and I carry all the burdens of shame, guilt, regret, remorse, and grief that comes with that. Trauma hurts. It hurts everyone around us. I hope she knows that I always love her unconditionally, and that I am so very sorry for the pain I caused her. I am sorry for not making her feel loved. I am sorry for not seeing her. I am sorry for not validating her. Simply, I am sorry.

In December, after such a difficult few years, I turned fifty. Knowing the pain and hurt I had endured, my circle of friends surrounded me with love and support and took me to Mexico to celebrate my birthday. But I was still in so much pain. Shortly thereafter, I was called by Spirit to get away on my own and go somewhere to heal and start writing my book. I decided on San Pedro, Belize. I had never been to the country of Belize, but I had family there that I had never met on my father's side. I was being called to go there. I went to Belize for the entire month of February in 2021. During that month, I worked on releasing my pain and suffering, met some wonderful people, and changed my perspective on life and what really matters. I wrote Jazmine another apology, trying once again to mend our broken relationship, but I had to leave the situation in her court. This was now her healing journey, and it had to be her decision to welcome me back into her life, or not. When I returned from my month-long stay in Belize, my friend Valerie's prediction came true: my business took off, went through the roof, and by April, I met my current partner, Noel. Life was about to completely change for me.

All these events gave me the faith and trust that I needed to keep going. I always tell my clients, "You've just got to go with the flow." Yes, things are going to happen, but if you continue to surrender, you can manage more successfully. Often, during challenging times, the Universe is removing things from our lives that don't support our highest good anymore.

Even though Jazmine and I are still estranged, I think the lesson for me was that everyone has their own perspective and their own lens-view. All I can do is own my part in those things that hurt others. All I can do is look at myself and at how others perceive me. It was time to do some serious self-reflection.

I needed to continue to work on myself. No matter how much I grow, I'm not perfect, and I have faults. I will make mistakes because I'm human, but I'm willing to go back and look and re-evaluate: *What part am I playing?*

Soul Lessons and Unconditional Love

Every soul signs up for different soul lessons before embarking on the life journey. Your soul's purpose is to reach unconditional love. Most of us have to learn how to love and accept people for who they are. We must learn forgiveness towards others and ourselves. It's about the soul's growth, not the ego's growth.

When we think of life as a series of soul lessons, we completely abandon the low-vibrational field of victimhood. That is, things aren't happening to us; they're happening *for* the benefit of our soul so that we grow as human beings. The ultimate goal is to reach a place of pure, unconditional love—even toward those who have hurt us.

We are all moving towards becoming more fully realized spiritual beings, but it takes many lifetimes of lessons for most of us. I continue to walk this lifetime learning forgiveness, love, and other important lessons that allow me to be of service to others.

Being the Beacon

As mediums, we can be beacons for people in different stages of pain, grief, and circumstance. Your light will help to cast out the darkness that surrounds others. You will be directed to their path to give them hope, permission to heal, and to offer tools to become fully empowered. It is your commitment to keep growing and learning spiritually that will help you make a difference in people's lives. I have compiled a few of my own client's stories to show you what a difference you can make to others. Like me, you do not have to be perfect—only willing and available to Spirit.

Following are a few examples of how you might shed light into the lives of others when you give yourself fully to being a medium.

There is deep suffering and trauma in the world. And you are needed.

Murdered: Finding Forgiveness in Tragedy

A woman named Shannon reached out to me last year for a reading. Shannon's female cousin was murdered by her nephew. He killed his mom, stepdad, and his four- and twelve-year-old siblings. It was on the news broadcasts in West Virginia; I think he was angry with his stepdad, and there may have been some abuse that nobody knew about. He came into the house and shot them all, starting with his mom and stepdad. The twelve-year-old heard the noise and came to the door, so he shot him, too. Then they found the younger child under a bed, also dead.

They lost so many at the hands of a relative, and there wasn't a stranger to be angry at. They are all still mending, trying to come to terms with the senseless tragedy while finding a path to forgiveness for the nephew who's in prison right now.

From Spirit's perspective, the mom still loves her son, even though things like this can happen. I encouraged them to search deep in their soul for forgiveness because they are family. The crime was committed by an adolescent who doesn't have a mind developed enough to see past the consequences. At seventeen years of age, he's not yet showing any remorse.

There's a reason that this happened. "There's a purpose for our pain," I tell them all the time. "There's a purpose for you. Perhaps you will write a book or counsel other young people who are suffering. There is truly a reason. It will become clearer with time."

The other survivors in the family are Shannon, her mother, and husband. I've done readings for all three of them. During my reading, most of what came out were things from the children's perspectives. The four-year-old kept talking about the stuffed animal that was given to him; apparently, they buried him with his favorite little stuffed, green, big-eared character from a space movie. The older boy did archery and was funny and outgoing. None of them in Spirit talked about the tragedy, but they said that they're all fine, and are together in the afterlife. Spirits commonly will focus less on the tragic occurrences and more on their present state and past information that offers evidence that they are communicating from the other side and that all is well.

I believe we have a plan before we even get here. When one returns to Heaven, or the other dimension, one's life plan is reviewed. You return home in a place of very high vibration and love—unconditional love. There's no hate; those are all earthly feelings, not Spirit feelings. But from a Spirit perspective, you have compassion and love. You see the bigger picture: you see what this is going to do to that little boy who is left here for the rest of his life. You see the pain and the anguish he's going to go through, so you can still find compassion for him now. Spirit's perspective is so different from ours.

You might be thinking, how was this healing for the family? How can a reading make such a difference when it comes to something as horrible as murder?

There is comfort and understanding in giving people proof of life after death, knowing that their loved ones really are still around as they give survivors signs that all is well. It does not take away the grief, but it plants the seeds of hope that there's more to this life than just this.

As people go through their grief, eventually they're going to find the magic. They're going to see these signs and feel at peace because of the understanding that they get to have their own direct connection to their beloveds. Once I have planted some seeds of hope into them that there is life after death, it often awakens their awareness so that they can get their own signs and can feel the deep comfort of being fully supported by Spirit.

Does it take away the pain?

No, but it offers hope.

I like to plant the seeds because I feel that this is what a mother would want. A mother wouldn't want her son to be all alone in this world anymore, right? Yes, he did something awful. But I always ask people.

"You're a mom or dad? How much do you love your children?"

I'll ask any mother: How much do you love your child? What if he or she went through a bad thing and hurt or killed somebody? Would you love the child any less? Or would you have compassion and try to figure out what happened? That's how God feels; we're all his children. As mediums, we offer the chance to look at tragedy and pain from a much larger lens.

My job is to help the sitter zoom out and see the bigger picture. Because I think that if you can see a larger perspective, from a soul level, it makes our tragedies easier to bear. How can we turn that pain into a purpose?

My job is to plant the seed that you can't walk this Earth with hate because it's just going to hurt you. It's going to cause disease in your own body. It's going to cause you to have a clouded perspective, not to trust, and to be angry.

So we're talking about vibration—if you stay in a low vibration, since like attracts like, you're going to attract bad things because you're stuck in a low vibration. Starting to heal and getting through the tragedy, and learning forgiveness, acceptance, and understanding, raises your vibration. The ultimate goal is unconditional love—and unconditional love means even loving someone who killed somebody. There's unconditional love as a soul, and as a human being—an understanding of what led to those events.

Shannon wrote to me after the reading, ". . . the peace I got from speaking to you was like they were here again! I cried happy tears and sad tears. Losing the boys and their mom is something I will never get over, but thanks to you I now have peace of mind, peace of heart. Just knowing they are well and all together makes me happy."

Death of a Child: I Can Still Hear You, Mom

Children's deaths are probably the hardest types of readings for most mediums, especially those of us who are also moms. You are going to have readings where people have lost a child or children. You will have miscarriages, stillbirths, babies, small children, teenagers, and young adults. One of the most memorable readings I have ever done was connecting a momma to her son who tragically passed away at the age of eighteen, and that's the Kate Muse story.

Her son, Terrance, had just graduated from high school. After a heated disagreement with his girlfriend, he sped angrily onto the country roads. He lost control and hit a tree, dying instantly. His mother, Kate, and her two daughters traveled from Alabama to see me, desperate for healing.

The first reading gave them comfort to know that it wasn't a suicide, because it was so questionable. His Spirit came through to explain that he was just a young man who could not handle his emotions, and he lost his focus as he revved the engine on the back roads of Alabama.

He told me that he was a football player back in high school—his glory days. The color red was important to him. His shoes were important. His music was important. He wanted me to tell his mother that he loved her. He offered all the evidence the family needed to know that he was there with them, still loving them.

The family booked another reading with me. Before they arrived, I went for a walk at a nearby nature preserve with a lake. I sat, just to connect with him, and said, "You know what? Give me something for your momma."

As I sat there on a rock, a huge monarch butterfly circled around me. It hovered at my side the whole time I was there. I took a photo of it. When I came back, and we were talking, I said, "Your son gave me a gift for you. He told me that you would know it was from him."

I showed her the photo, and she began crying. "Oh my! That *is* him."

She explained that they live in the countryside, and he's buried in their backyard, under a big, beautiful tree. In honor of his memory, the family painted butterflies on its branches.

Terrance in Spirit ended the reading by saying, "Tell my mom that the check's in the mail."

She just started laughing and said, "I don't think he means that literally. You see, he would always tell me, 'Mom, go check the mail. See if there's a check waiting for you! You never know . . . there might just be!'" She was a single mom who was struggling all the time—and his words were a loving way for him to say, "Don't lose the faith. Keep believing good things are on the way."

The last reading was in December. She wanted it on his birthday. He talked about the food she was making for his birthday. She made meatloaf, his favorite dish. She had balloon bouquets hanging from the rafters, letting him know how special he was to them.

I can't bring him back, but I can tell her that what she's hearing is real, and that she can still talk to him. I can reassure that he's watching over everyone, giving her hope that it's not the end. When our beloveds pass away, and they are void of their bodies and no longer here, the essence of who they are is still with us, and we can still connect with them.

I reminded Kate, as I do with all my sitters: "You'll just have a *different* kind of a relationship now, that's all."

Suicide: So Sorry for All I Put You Through

Kristina and I met for lunch one day after she lost her husband Joshua to suicide. She was angry and devastated as she struggled to adjust to a life without him. I immediately felt Joshua's presence, desperate to tell Kristina, "I am sorry." Over and over again, I heard his words, "I am sorry for everything I put you through."

He was funny, silly, charming, able to tell a joke about anything, and clearly still loved her. He talked about his own childhood trauma with abuse in the church and his self-destructive tendencies throughout his life. Josh taught me that the souls of those who complete suicide don't go to some dark, fiery place; on the contrary, they experience the unconditional love and support of the afterlife. God, Source, Universe, whatever you would like to call the Higher Power, understands mental illness. There is nothing but love to welcome them to the other side. Joshua was able to share this abundant love with Kristina. While she still, of course, deeply mourned his loss, she also learned that day that love is eternal. Joshua would always be with her.

Abuse

You will undoubtedly have people who have been abused either sexually, physically, or mentally by someone who has passed away.

Often, souls want to come through to apologize to their victims. These readings can be extremely difficult depending on where your sitter is in the healing process. Spirit may be ready to apologize, but your sitter may not be ready, able, or willing to hear it. It's important to honor where everyone is in their healing process. If an abuser comes through and the sitter is not ready, end the connection. You never want to cause more harm or trauma to your sitter. Be cautious, always.

C.B. booked a reading with me to reconnect with her grandfather. During the reading, I kept getting another grandfather trying to come through. Every time I mentioned something about this grandfather, C.B. would shut down a little. As I read her energy, I had a clear sense that this was an abuse situation. I asked C.B. if she wanted me to end the connection with him. She said, with her head hung down, "Yes, he abused me, and I do not want to hear from him."

Of course, I honored her wishes and ended contact with him immediately. Instead, I reinforced my connection with her other grandfather. She had fond memories of fishing with him. He would collect coins, and she loved looking at all of them while he lovingly explained the history and origins of each one. He was the grandfather she loved and trusted. That was the grandfather she wanted to remember, to bring through.

Parental Loss

Amanda came to me for a reading after the passing of her mother in early 2020. She was filled with sadness and having a really hard time moving past her grief. She had suffered a lot of loss with the passing of her dad, dog, and then her mother. I was able to connect right away with her dad, and his cowboy hat that he would always wear.

He let Amanda know how much he approved of her husband and that he was at her wedding in Spirit. "He wouldn't have missed it for the world." He knew that she had placed a picture of him at a table set for family who was no longer with us anymore. He also told her he "loved" who she picked to walk her down the aisle in his place . . . her twin brother. Dad also mentioned the dog she had lost was with him. Mom then came through with apologies for not always being the best mom she could have been. She thanked Amanda for taking care of her expenses and being there until the end for her. It was very heart-touching, and I felt the shift in Amanda's energy after the reading was over. She had hope. Her mindset had instantly shifted. She was ready to heal. She explained to me, "My reading put me on the path to loving and forgiving myself."

Denise, who also had a reading after losing her parents, shared: ". . . My reading helped me move forward in my grieving process by accepting that my parents are no longer here, but I can still talk to them and receive reminders that they're close by and still listening."

And the Bankston family wrote me one day: ". . . Losing our father, the patriarch of our family, was devastating. When he came through during our reading and gave us the thumbs up, we all started to cry. That was our sign during the funeral to each other.

We knew then that he approved of the funeral and how we honored him."

Love Interrupted: When a Soul Mate Passes On

Can you imagine the loss of a soul mate—the person you were supposed to spend the rest of your life with? I have encountered many clients who had to experience the death of their lover, best friend, soul mate. It can be gut-wrenching. Future plans suddenly mean nothing. Every night, an empty bed is a haunting reminder of the loss. The phone no longer rings with the beloved's words. Losing one's soul mate can leave the surviving partner with no hopes or desire of ever loving again.

Mattie reached out to me three weeks after she lost her boyfriend, her soul mate. She had come home from work and found him on the floor of their apartment. At the time of our reading, she did not know his cause of death but did suspect an overdose. She had so many questions. Was she to blame? Should she have seen this coming? Did this mean he wasn't happy? Did she do something wrong? What if she hadn't worked that day? His death was such a shock and completely stopped her world at the time. She desperately wished she could talk to him one more time and ask him all these questions. She wanted to know if he was scared in his last moments. Could he hear her when she cried for him at night?

I started our conversation letting her know that since I was sensing that his passing was recent, he may not come through strongly. Well, I was wrong! I immediately received information that his passing was sudden and unexpected. He gave me the initial "B."

(His name was Brandon.) He spoke of "the thing she was looking at with his writing in it." Mattie had his journal sitting next to her during our reading. Brandon also talked about shoes under the bed, and he had a pair of work shoes there. Brandon also talked about a memorial tattoo on an arm. Mattie and Brandon's brother had tattoos engraved in his memory.

Brandon spoke of his grandfather who met him at his time of death and helped him transition. He was not scared or hurting, and he knew his whole family and her were there with him before they took his body away. He told me he was in a place of unconditional love, and that he could hear Mattie when she talked to him. He spoke of his kind and gentle heart and his great love for his family. The gift of bringing Spirit into the lives of others is, as Mattie described, "like shining a light in such a dark time in my life. I am forever grateful . . . ."

Finding Purpose in Your Pain

A natural response to pain is to look away, turn a blind eye, stuff feelings and emotions, deny it ever happened, and compartmentalize. If we do not confront our pain, it can cause long-term health and/or mental problems. Many suffer from anxiety, panic attacks, depression, substance abuse, sleep disorders, isolation, hopelessness, physical disease, or ailments.

When we are faced with pain and have the ability to confront it and understand what purpose pain has in our life, we can begin to find the positives, the lessons, the significance behind our suffering.

"What could possibly be the meaning for my pain?" you may be asking yourself at this moment. Let me help give you a different perspective.

- Pain can be the catalyst of self-reflection on life choices.
- Pain can give you compassion and empathy for others.
- Pain can inspire you.
- Pain can cause you to take action.
- Pain can cause you to seek out gratitude.
- Pain can help you to seek out healthier boundaries, habits, and relationships.

Finding the purpose in your pain is a key part of the entire healing process. It's not about the "why" it happened—it's about how you choose to live with your painful experience. You can be crushed and debilitated by it, or you can find purpose in it.

The path I walked during this lifetime was not an easy one. I lived thirty-plus years in survival mode. I faced death, addiction, abuse, self-destructive behavior, a lack of self-worth, and lack of self-love. My soul was crying out for help. My soul was begging me to heal.

I can't explain the supernatural energy that came over me in late 2015. Divine intervention? Possibly. I like to explain it to others that Spirit swooped down and wrapped its arms around me and said, "No more suffering; trust us to lead the way."

From that point on, they began to make me aware of all the synchronicities I had missed in my misery: How the color red, like the dress I wore to my father's funeral at the age of nineteen, would become so significant in my life. How a vision of a red couch in the woods would be foreshadowing my future purpose. How finding a red couch in a pasture weeks later would lead me to finding a purpose for my years of pain.

The red couch encounter forced me to see that there was more to the Earth plane than I could ever imagine. There was magic in a world that I only saw as painful. I learned that I was not meant to suffer. I could be the observer of my experiences and not be defined by them.

The red couch has been the biggest influence in my journey to mediumship. Often, Spirit will place one in my path to keep me encouraged to keep going—to let me know I am walking the path I was always meant to walk. I am humbled by the great life I have now as I live my purpose. Now I understand the reasons for my pain and guide others to do the same.

We are not meant to live a life of suffering. We are meant to have lessons that enable our soul's growth and provide us with contrast. I encourage you to find your "red couch"—that symbol or sign that inspires you to blossom and reach for the light.

Find your purpose in the pain—then you will be able to cultivate a garden of goodness that will bloom, sending beauty and joy into the world.

Made in the USA
Las Vegas, NV
15 December 2022

62733384R00155